FORK, SPOON
AND FINGER FOOD

FORK, SPOON AND FINGER FOOD

Catherine Althaus
and
Peter ffrench-Hodges

FABER AND FABER LIMITED
3 Queen Square London

First published in 1975
by Faber and Faber Limited
3 Queen Square London WC1
Printed in Great Britain
by Latimer Trend & Company Ltd Plymouth

ISBN 0 571 10613 7

CONTENTS

CONTENTS

INTRODUCTION

This book is about today's way of eating and entertaining. The grand buffets of yesterday with long tables laden with food can still be seen in hotels and at weddings and other celebrations, but they rarely have a place in the modern household.

We suggest you push the table to the wall and let down the wings if it's that kind of table, to give space for people.

We are writing for those who want good food without fuss and for modern people of all ages for whom space is at a premium.

The art of entertaining is for you to be relaxed and for the atmosphere to be relaxing for your guests. The easiest way to achieve this is to forget about dining room conventions and formality. Eat off your knees or from any available space—but for this to be enjoyable for your guests, it has to be made easy and comfortable for them. It is for this reason that every recipe in this book can be eaten with one hand—i.e. with fingers, spoon or fork. At a party there are few things more exasperating than having to balance a glass, and at the same time, try to cut one's way through a large piece of meat. Another advantage of this informal and relaxed way of entertaining is that your guests can move round at will and talk to different people.

As this book is written for the modern cook who is likely to be already familiar with metrication, quantities are given in metric measurements with the avoirdupois to the nearest ounce or fraction of a pint in brackets, so anyone who is still finding metrication a mystery will be able to use the book while adapting to the new system; this will become essential as food becomes available in metric quantities only. It is not possible to be 100 per cent accurate using both sets of measurements concurrently, but you will find on p. 15 our own conversion table to which each recipe has been worked. This may not tally with other metrication tables you have, but each recipe in this book has been worked out to this scale, so that you will get perfect results using either the metric or the avoirdupois measurements, but you should avoid a mixture of the two.

Fork, Spoon and Finger Food is divided into four sections: Appetizers, Beginnings, Mains and Afters. Each recipe is marked to show whether it can be successfully frozen. In the Appendix you will find a few basic notes on freezing, but we have already dealt with deep freezing in some detail in our *Freeze Now, Dine Later*. Dishes are also marked as to whether or not they can be prepared in advance.

We give recipes for hot and cold food which can be enjoyed both for parties and for everyday meals. The section on appetizers is designed rather more with a party in mind, when we suggest you may like to serve a selection of two or three hot or cold appetizers with pre-dinner drinks, rather than having a Beginnings. This cuts down on the necessary equipment, as all the food in this section is designed to be eaten in the fingers.

There is never any excuse for waste, so trust your own judgement and keep your selection of food simple. Just because your friends are serving themselves, it doesn't mean they have to have a larger selection of dishes from which to choose. Be courageous with your food and the ways of serving it. Don't apologize for your decisions by backing them up with alternatives; don't spoil a one-handed meal with two-handed concessions. Don't allow juices to go to waste, and if you prepare a main course with a very runny consistency, invite your friends to eat it with a spoon out of a bowl.

Presentation, always important, is even more so when people are helping themselves, so do pay a lot of attention to this. One dish plonked down on the table looks dull, if not downright uninviting. So have small bowls of flowers for decoration, using where possible colours that will complement your china and food. Never over garnish food, but make sure it is presented in the most attractive dish you have, and that you have made it look as appetizing as possible. Brightly coloured paper napkins help to make a buffet table inviting. Lighting is an important factor too. No one likes sitting under bright lights, and candles can be a most attractive addition to an evening buffet table, but remember that people like to see what they are eating.

Try not to produce food too soon or too long after your guests arrive. They should welcome the meal naturally, rather than feel it is thrust upon them hurriedly, or held back until they cease to care.

We hope the recipes in this book will not only make entertaining easier, but will also add to the daily enjoyment of good food.

GENERAL NOTES ON THE USE OF THIS BOOK

1. *Quantities* All quantities are sufficient for 8 people.

2. *Freezing* Each recipe is marked as to whether it may be successfully frozen. Basic rules on freezing will be found in Appendix III.

3. *Preparation in advance* Dishes are marked as to whether they can be successfully prepared in advance. Some dishes are marked 'Suitable for advance preparation'. This means they may be prepared in full, and reheated or garnished at the last moment as is appropriate. Some are marked 'Can be prepared in advance until . . .'. This means that you may prepare the recipe in advance until the beginning of the appropriate action number, i.e. 'until 4' means up to the end of action 3. It is important that when dishes are to be prepared in advance, they should be cooled completely, then kept refrigerated and, on reheating, they should be brought to bubbling point and maintained at that heat for 10 minutes. The garnish should be added at the point of serving. Some recipes are not suitable for advance preparation at all and should be cooked at the last minute. These are marked 'Not suitable for advance preparation'.

4. *Dry measurements* The measurements for dry quantities are given in kilogrammes (kg.) and grammes (g.), with the nearest pound (lb.) and ounce (oz.) equivalent given beside them in brackets. These comparisons have been calculated according to the table on p. 15. The metric and avoirdupois quantities should not be mixed.

5. *Liquid measurements* The measurements for liquid quantities are given in litres and deci-litres (dl.), with the nearest equivalent in pints or fractions thereof given afterwards in brackets. Again these two forms of measurement should not be mixed. A table of liquid measurements will be found on p. 17.

6. *Stock* Except where a 'strong' stock is called for, you can substitute stock made up with either a chicken or a meat cube, in

13

any of the recipes that follow. Appendix I gives directions for making stock.

7. *Flour*   Except where self-raising flour is specifically mentioned, all flour used in the recipes is plain.

8. *Pastry*   These days, many people prefer to buy their pastry ready-made, fresh or frozen. When you are making your own, you will need to adjust the ingredients to produce the weight of pastry called for in the recipe. This is an easy matter with plain shortcrust where half a pound of flour and a quarter pound of fat will produce approximately three-quarters of a pound of pastry. With pastries containing other ingredients, such as sugar, egg yolk or cheese, a very little practice will enable you to arrive at the amounts called for in the recipes. Directions for making pastry are in Appendix I.

9. *Herbs and seasonings*   Fresh herbs are naturally better than dried ones, but on account of the difficulty of obtaining fresh herbs, dried may be substituted, except where fresh herbs are specifically mentioned. It should be noted that smaller quantities of fresh herbs are needed as they have a more pungent flavour before they are dried. Frozen herbs may also be substituted.

Dried herbs and some seasonings lose their flavour if kept too long.

Some recipes call for seasoning with lemon pepper. This can be found in some speciality shops and it is well worth searching for.

10. *Banging meat*   Where a recipe calls for you to bang the meat flat, the simplest method is to put it in a polythene bag, rather than the traditional method of between sheets of wet paper. In this way you can see exactly what you are doing.

11. *Appetizers*   The section on appetizers contains recipes for food designed to be eaten in the fingers. We suggest you may like to serve a selection of hot or cold appetizers with pre-meal drinks, instead of having a beginnings, thereby saving eating utensils and washing up.

12. *Vegetable sizes*   We have only specified the size of tomatoes, peppers, onions, potatoes etc. when the size is relevant to the recipe; otherwise we mean medium-sized.

METRIC CONVERSION TABLES

Measurements for Rounded Tablespoons

1 tablespoon castor sugar = $\frac{3}{4}$ oz. = 20 g.
1 tablespoon flour   = 1   oz. = 30 g.
1 tablespoon butter   = $1\frac{1}{4}$ oz. = 35 g.
1 tablespoon cornflour = $\frac{1}{2}$ oz. = 15 g.
1 tablespoon gelatin   = $\frac{3}{4}$ oz. = 20 g.

Roux-Based Sauces

Thin Sauce	1 oz. flour	1 oz. butter	1 pint liquid
	30 g. flour	30 g. butter	6 dl. liquid
Medium Sauce	2 oz. flour	2 oz. butter	1 pint liquid
	60 g. flour	60 g. butter	6 dl. liquid
Thick Sauce	3 oz. flour	3 oz. butter	1 pint liquid
	85 g. flour	85 g. butter	6 dl. liquid

Dry Measurements Conversion Table from which All Recipes in this Book have been Calculated

Ounces	Grammes	Ounces	Grammes
$\frac{1}{4}$	5	9	250 ($\frac{1}{4}$ kg.)
$\frac{1}{2}$	15	10	280
$\frac{3}{4}$	20	11	310
1	30	12 ($\frac{3}{4}$ lb.)	335
2	60	13	365
3	85	14	390
4 ($\frac{1}{4}$ lb.)	110	15	420
5	140	16 (1 lb.)	450
6	170	17	475
7	195	18	500 ($\frac{1}{2}$ kg.)
8 ($\frac{1}{2}$ lb.)	220	19	530

B

Ounces	Grammes	Ounces	Grammes
20 (1¼ lb.)	560	28 (1¾ lb.)	785
21	590	29	810
22	615	30	840
23	645	31	870
24 (1½ lb.)	670	32 (2 lb.)	900
25	700	33	925
26	730	34	952
27	750 (¾ kg.)	35¾ (2¼ lb.)	1,000 (1 kg.)

Pounds and Ounces	Kilogrammes	Grammes
2½		1,110
2¾	1¼	1,250
3		1,350
3¼	1½	1,500
3½		1,570
3¾		1,680
3	14	1¾	1,750
4		1,790
4¼		1,900
4½	2	2,000

Liquid Measurements Conversion Table

Pints	Litres	Decilitres
¼		1½
⅓	(⅕)	2
½		3
⅔	(⅖)	4
¾		4½
⅚	(½)	5
1	(⅗)	6
1¼		7
1⅓	(⅘)	8
1½		9
1⅔	1	0 (10)

Pints	Litres	Decilitres
$1\frac{3}{4}$	1 and $\frac{1}{2}$ (10$\frac{1}{2}$)	
2	$1\frac{1}{5}$	
$2\frac{1}{4}$	$1\frac{1}{3}$	
$2\frac{1}{2}$	$1\frac{1}{2}$	
$2\frac{3}{4}$	$1\frac{3}{5}$	
3	$1\frac{3}{4}$	
$3\frac{1}{4}$	2	
$3\frac{1}{2}$	$2\frac{1}{5}$	
$3\frac{3}{4}$	$2\frac{1}{4}$	
4	$2\frac{2}{5}$	
5	3	

Table of Comparative Oven Temperatures

GAS OVEN SETTINGS	ELECTRIC OVEN SETTINGS Fahrenheit	Centigrade	
$\frac{1}{4}$	225°	110°	⎫
$\frac{1}{2}$	250°	130°	⎬ Very Slow
1	275°	140°	⎭
2	300°	150°	⎫ Slow
3	325°	160°	⎭
4	350°	180°	Very Moderate
5	375°	190°	Moderate
6	400°	200°	⎫ Moderately Hot
7	425°	220°	⎭
8	450°	230°	Hot
9	475°	240°	Very Hot

Note: An oven thermometer is recommended for cookers which have been converted to Natural Gas.

APPETIZERS

Cold

Nine Variations on a Stuffed Egg
8 large eggs per recipe

Fillings

1. 7·5cm. (3 in.) cucumber
   85 g. (3 oz.) Philadelphia
   cheese
   pepper
2. 4 rashers bacon
   3 small tomatoes
   pepper
3. 110 g. (¼ lb.) pâté (p. 25)
   1 tablespoon mayonnaise
   (p. 201)
   pepper
4. 60 g. (2 oz.) peeled prawns
   85 g. (3 oz.) Philadelphia
   cheese
   seasoning
5. 110 g. (¼ lb.) crab pâté
   1 tablespoon mayonnaise
   (p. 201)
   seasoning
6. 85 g. (3 oz.) smoked
   haddock
   1 tablespoon mayonnaise
   (p. 201)
   seasoning
7. 3–4 sardines
   1 tablespoon mayonnaise
   (p. 201)
   seasoning
8. 1 dessertspoon curry powder
   2 tablespoons mayonnaise
   (p. 201)
   seasoning
9. 2 teaspoons anchovy
   essence
   2 tablespoons mayonnaise
   (p. 201)
   pepper

Preparation

For all the recipes, hard boil the eggs. Cool and peel. Cut in half
and scoop out the yolks. Cut a little piece off the bottom of the
white so that they stand flat.

Action: Making the Fillings

1. Peel and crush the cucumber and mix with the cheese and
   yolks. Season with black pepper.
2. Cut rinds from bacon and crisply fry in its own fat. When
   cooked, crumble. Peel and purée the tomatoes. Mix both
   together with the yolks and season with black pepper.

21

3. Mix together the pâté and yolks, and moisten with the mayonnaise. Season.

4. Chop the prawns and mix with the cheese and yolks, moistening with the mayonnaise. Season.

5. Mix the crab pâté with the yolks and moisten with the mayonnaise. Season.

6. Wash the haddock, then poach in water or milk. Flake and mix with the mayonnaise and yolks. Season.

7. Extract the bones and mash the sardines with the yolks. Moisten with the mayonnaise and season.

8. Mix the curry with the mayonnaise and then mash with the yolks and seasoning.

9. Mix together the anchovy essence, mayonnaise and yolks. Season with pepper.

To Complete

For all the recipes, pile the filling back into the egg whites and garnish attractively.

Not suitable for freezing.

Can be prepared a few hours in advance. Filling 1 loses its flavour if prepared more than 2 hours before eating.

Note: Eggs can be stuffed with almost any left-over meat or fish, but the really important thing is that they should be moist, so add as much mayonnaise as is necessary to achieve this.

Hot

Camembert Moons

1 French loaf   60 g. (2 oz.) flaked almonds
220 g. (½ lb.) Camembert cheese

Preparation

Cut the loaf in half lengthways and repeat with the halves. Slice the bread across so that you have chunky quarter moons. Scoop out the crumbs.

Action

1. Press small pieces of Camembert into the bread crusts, then stick the almond slices into the cheese.
2. Place on a piece of foil in a baking tin and put into a hot oven for 5 minutes. Some of the cheese will inevitably run on to the foil, so don't worry when this happens.

Only suitable for freezing before cooking.

Can be prepared a few hours in advance, then cooked at the last moment.

Cold

Nut Truffle

335 g. (¾ lb.) Philadelphia cheese
110 g. (¼ lb.) ham

85 g. (3 oz.) stuffed olives
85 g. (3 oz.) blanched almonds
seasoning

Preparation

Finely chop the ham and the olives. Crush the almonds.

Action

Mix the ham and olives with the cheese and season. Roll the mixture into small balls which can easily be eaten in one mouthful and then roll them in the crushed almonds.

Suitable for freezing.

Can be prepared in advance.

Cold

Smoked Buckling Pâté

1–2 smoked buckling (220 g. (½ lb.) approx.)
110 g. (¼ lb.) butter

2 tablespoons oil
2 tablespoons lemon juice
seasoning

Preparation

Skin the buckling and extract any bones.

Action

Finely mash together the buckling, butter, oil and lemon juice.
Season to taste. Pack into ramekin dishes and chill until required.
Serve on crackers or fingers of brown bread and butter.

Suitable for freezing.

Can be prepared in advance.

Cold

Smoked Mackerel and Gooseberry Pâté

2 smoked mackerel	1 tablespoon water
220 g. (½ lb.) gooseberries	1 heaped tablespoon castor
60 g. (2 oz.) butter	sugar
1 tablespoon Calvados	freshly ground black pepper

Preparation

Skin the mackerel and fillet carefully, removing any bones. Wash,
top and tail gooseberries. Take the butter from the refrigerator to
soften.

Action

1. Place the gooseberries, sugar and water in a saucepan. Stir
   over a gentle heat to prevent burning. Simmer gently until the
   gooseberries are soft—about 10 minutes.

2. Purée the gooseberries in a blender and leave to cool.

3. Mash the fish very finely with the butter and Calvados, and
   when the gooseberries are cold blend them into the mixture and
   season with black pepper. Put the pâté into a dish to set, and
   keep in the refrigerator until required. Serve on plain buttered
   savoury biscuits, or on fingers of buttered toast.

Suitable for freezing for a short period.

Can be prepared in advance.

Cold

Chicken Liver Pâté

335 g. (¾ lb.) chicken livers	1 dessertspoon brandy
3 rashers streaky bacon	1 dessertspoon port
2 small onions	seasoning
140 g. (5 oz.) butter	

Preparation

Remove any skin or fat from the chicken livers. Cut the rinds off the bacon and cut the bacon into strips. Peel and finely chop the onions.

Action

1. Put the bacon and the rinds in a frying-pan and cook over a low heat.
2. When the fat has run out of the bacon, add the onions and chicken livers, and cook them lightly for 5 minutes. (Use a little of the butter if the bacon has not produced enough fat.)
3. Extract the bacon rinds, then put the contents of the frying-pan into a blender or Mouli. Add the butter, brandy, port and seasoning and mix until smooth.
4. Turn the pâté into a dish, and leave to set in the refrigerator until required. Serve on crackers or fingers of toast.

Suitable for freezing.

Can be prepared in advance.

Cold

Prune Pâté

6 vacuum-packed stoned prunes	1 slice white bread
335 g. (¾ lb.) chicken livers	110 g. (¼ lb.) butter
60 g. (2 oz.) bacon rind	1 dl. (⅙ pint) red wine
110 g. (¼ lb.) ham	1 tablespoon chopped parsley
1 small onion	seasoning

Preparation

Remove any skin or fat from the chicken livers. Slice the prunes into small pieces. Peel and finely chop the onion. Soften the butter.

Action

1. Put the bacon rinds in a frying-pan and heat for 3 minutes so that the fat runs out.
2. In this fat sauté the onion and the chicken livers, adding up to one-eighth of the butter if the bacon does not produce sufficient fat. Turn the chicken livers, cooking them for 5 minutes each side.
3. Discard the bacon rind.* Cool the onion and livers and put them in a bowl with the wine, bread, ham, parsley and seasoning. Mix roughly together and put through a mincer.
4. Add the softened butter and the finely chopped prunes and chill. Serve on small pieces of crusty new bread.

Suitable for freezing.

Can be prepared in advance.

Note: Crisp bacon rinds are very good as an appetizer.

Cold

Pork Pâté Hubs

335 g. (¾ lb.) leg of pork	1 dl. (⅙ pint) dry vermouth
110 g. (¼ lb.) chicken livers	½ teaspoon basil
1 small onion	¼ teaspoon thyme
4 cloves garlic	seasoning
1 slice white bread	1 French loaf
1 tablespoon oil	

Preparation

Remove any skin or fat from the chicken livers. Cut the fat from the pork and reserve. Peel and rough chop the onion. Peel the garlic. Cut the crust off the slice of white bread.

26

Action

1. Sauté the chicken livers in the oil for 10 minutes. Cool.
2. Put the pork, chicken livers, onion, garlic and white bread through a mincer.
3. Add the herbs, seasoning and vermouth. Place in a fire-proof dish and lay the pork fat on top. Put the dish inside a larger one containing water which should rise to the level of the meat inside the first dish. Bake in a moderate oven for 1½ hours. Cool.
4. Slice the French bread and remove the crumb from the centre of each crust. Remove the pork fat from the top of the pâté and discard. Fill the round crusts with the pâté.

Suitable for freezing before putting into the French bread.

Can be prepared in advance until 4.

Hot

Orange Fried Fish

670 g. (1½ lb.) fillet of plaice	1½ dl. (¼ pint) milk
2 large oranges	seasoning
1 egg	oil for deep frying
170 g. (6 oz.) flour	

Preparation

Cut each fillet into 5 or 6 pieces. Finely grate the peel of one whole orange and half of the other. Cut the oranges in half and squeeze the juice from 3 of the 4 halves, the reserved half being the one with the peel intact. Cut this into half moons for decoration.

Action

1. Heat the oil in a deep frying-pan.
2. Make a heavy batter, breaking the egg into the flour, mixing it well in, and then stirring in the milk and orange juice. Beat well. Add the grated orange peel and seasoning.
3. Dip the fish in the batter and fry until golden. Be careful to keep the individual pieces apart, otherwise they will join together as they cook. Serve speared with a cocktail stick.

Not suitable for freezing.

Can be prepared in advance and kept warm in the oven for up to 1 hour.

Hot

Soft Roe Vol-au-Vents

20 small commercially frozen
 vol-au-vent cases
¼ kg. (9 oz.) soft herring roes
2 tablespoons oil
45 g. (1½ oz.) butter
45 g. (1½ oz.) flour

4 dl. (⅔ pint) milk
1 dl. (⅙ pint) sherry
½ teaspoon lemon pepper
seasoned flour (p. 198)
seasoning

Preparation

Remove the vol-au-vent cases from the freezer and leave them at room temperature for 30 minutes. Wash the roes and coat well with seasoned flour.

Action

1. Cook the vol-au-vents in a moderate oven for 20 minutes.
2. Sauté the roes in the oil for 10 minutes, turning them so that they are brown on each side. Cool and chop.
3. Make a white sauce with the butter, flour and milk (p. 203). When the sauce has boiled for 4 minutes, add the sherry and the chopped roes. Add the lemon pepper and other seasoning and allow to cool.
4. When the vol-au-vents are cooked, remove from the oven, and with a pointed knife lift out the centre caps and reserve. Scrape out any loose pastry and discard.
5. Fill the cases with the roe mixture and replace caps on top. Return to the oven for 10 minutes.

Not suitable for freezing.

Can be prepared in advance until 5. They can be kept warm in a very slow oven for up to 40 minutes if necessary.

Hot

Smoked Cod's Roe Vol-au-Vents

20 small commercially frozen   45 g. (1½ oz.) flour
  vol-au-vent cases   4 dl. (⅔ pint) milk
110 g. (4 oz.) smoked cod's roe   1 dl. (⅙ pint) red wine
60 g. (2 oz.) peeled prawns   seasoning
45 g. (1½ oz.) butter

Preparation

Remove the vol-au-vents from the freezer and leave at room temperature for 30 minutes. Put the smoked cod's roe through a mincer, having first removed the skin.

Action

1. Put the vol-au-vents to cook in a moderate oven for 20 minutes.
2. Make a white sauce with the butter, flour and milk (p. 203). When the sauce has boiled for 4 minutes, add the wine and the smoked cod's roe. Season and allow to cool.
3. When the vol-au-vents are cooked, take them from the oven, and with a pointed knife lift out the centre caps and reserve. Scrape out any loose pastry and discard.
4. Place 2 prawns in each of the vol-au-vent cases, and pour over the sauce. Replace the caps and return the vol-au-vents to the oven for 10 minutes.

Not suitable for freezing.

Can be prepared in advance until 4. They can be kept warm in a very slow oven for up to 40 minutes if necessary.

Hot

Fried Fish Balls

280 g. (10 oz.) cod fillet   seasoned flour (p. 198)
110 g. (¼ lb.) peeled prawns   seasoning
140 g. (5 oz.) self-raising flour oil for deep frying
1 tablespoon tomato ketchup

Preparation

Remove any skin from the cod. Break the fish into flakes, searching for bones.

Action

1. Heat the oil in a deep frying-pan.
2. Combine the cod, prawns, flour and tomato ketchup. Season. Divide into 20 pieces and roll into balls.
3. Roll the balls in seasoned flour and fry until golden in the very hot oil.

Suitable for freezing.

Can be prepared a few hours in advance and reheated in the oven.

Hot or cold

Curry Puffs

1 small tin Le Ka Ri mild   335 g. (¾ lb.) flaky pastry
  Malayan curry   (p. 196)
110 g. (¼ lb.) peeled prawns or   milk or egg for glazing
  minced left-over meat

Preparation

Cut the prawns in half. Roll out the pastry thinly, then cut out into circles about 7·5 cm. (3 in.) in diameter.

Action

1. Tip the curry into a bowl and mix in the meat or fish.
2. Place a little of the curry stuffing in the middle of each piece of pastry. Dampen the edges of the pastry and press together well to enclose the filling, then buff up the edges with the back of a knife.
3. Place the puffs so that they are not touching on a baking sheet. Brush with a little milk or lightly beaten egg to give a glaze. Bake in a hot oven for about 15 minutes, until golden.

Suitable for freezing, but preferably before baking.

Can be prepared in advance.

Cold

Chicken Sausage

1 medium chicken	1 thick slice white bread
110 g. (¼ lb.) chicken livers	1 tablespoon oil
2 eggs	¼ teaspoon basil
1 small onion	pinch of thyme
4 cloves garlic	seasoning

Preparation

Remove any skin or fat from the chicken livers. Bone the chicken, but do not skin. Beat the eggs. Peel and chop the onion. Peel the garlic.

Action

1. Sauté the chicken livers with the onion in the oil for 10 minutes. Cool. Do not wash the frying-pan.

2. Put the chicken, chicken livers, onions, garlic and bread through a mincer. Mix the ingredients together and put through the mincer again. Season and add the herbs. Mix in the beaten eggs.

3. Tie the mixture in a muslin cloth, the shape of a fat sausage and poach in water in the unwashed frying-pan for 1 hour. Cool and slice. Serve on crackers.

Suitable for freezing.

Can be prepared in advance.

Hot

Chicken Rolls

4 half chicken breasts	1½ dl. (¼ pint) double cream
110 g. (¼ lb.) chicken livers	⅛ teaspoon ground nutmeg
8 bread rolls	seasoning
1½ dl. (¼ pint) milk	

C
31

Preparation

Cut the chicken from the bone and discard the skin. Remove any skin or fat from the chicken livers. Slice the rolls in half lengthways, so that they open but don't break in half. Scoop out the crumb so that only the shells remain.

Action

1. Finely mince the chicken and the chicken livers and put in a covered pan with the milk and the nutmeg. Season. Cook over a moderate heat for 15 minutes, stirring occasionally. Warm the rolls in the oven.
2. Drain off the liquid. Add the cream and stir over the heat until hot, but not boiling. Spoon the mixture into the rolls.

Suitable for freezing separately.

Not suitable for advance preparation.

Cold

Brie Chicken

4 half chicken breasts
220 g. (½ lb.) failed brie
  cheese*

⅛ teaspoon basil
seasoning

Preparation

Remove the skin and bone from the chicken and beat flat. Scrape the outside of the brie with a serrated knife to remove the white rind, then split lengthways like a sandwich.

Action

1. Sprinkle the basil and seasoning over the chicken and grill under a moderate fire for about 5 minutes on each side.
2. Place the brie over the chicken so that it is completely covered, and grill for a further 8 minutes, until the cheese has melted and turned light brown. Cool.
3. When cool, cut into squares.

Not suitable for freezing.

Can be prepared a few hours in advance.

Note: This is a delicious way of using failed brie (i.e. one which has failed to ripen) which would otherwise have to be thrown away. Obviously you are unlikely to be unfortunate enough to find yourself with so much all at once, but the brie will keep in the freezer, so you can add to your supply until you have the required amount.

Cold

Fillet Tomatoes

335 g. (¾ lb.) best fillet steak	*For the Béarnaise Sauce*
10 large tomatoes	5 egg yolks
8 approx. tablespoons	195 g. (7 oz.) butter
Béarnaise sauce	2 shallots
seasoning	3 tablespoons wine vinegar
	2 tablespoons water
	1 teaspoon tarragon
	seasoning

Preparation

Trim any fat from the meat. Cut the tops off 8 of the tomatoes and scoop out the insides. With scissors cut new moons from the top for decoration.

Action

1. Make the béarnaise sauce (p. 205). Cool.
2. Put the steak in a hot frying-pan without any oil or butter and cook for 2 minutes each side. Cool. Break into 8 pieces with your fingers. If you have to resort to a knife, then the steak is not tender enough.
3. Put the divided steak in the tomatoes with a little seasoning and surround with béarnaise sauce, piling some on top into which you stick the tomato new moons.
4. The remaining 2 tomatoes are for decoration. Make an incision across the base of each as if you were about to slice off

a piece the size of a 1p. piece, but instead of cutting right through, alter the angle of the knife as it reaches the far skin and peel the tomato instead, trying to maintain an even 1p. width of peel all the time. Place the peel on its base piece and curl it around itself. You have a rose.

Not suitable for freezing.

Can be prepared 1 hour in advance.

Cold

Mango Bacon

20 rashers back bacon   140 g. (5 oz.) cottage cheese
2 large mangoes   seasoning

Preparation

Cut the rind off the bacon. Peel the mangoes and slice bite-size chunks from the fruit, working around the stone, until the flesh becomes stringy. Each mango should provide ten pieces.

Action

Grill the bacon until it just begins to go crisp. Cool and wrap around the mango. Season and seal the bacon wrap with a blob of cottage cheese.

Not suitable for freezing.

Can be prepared a few hours in advance.

Cold

Salami Boats

20 slices wide Danish Salami   1 dessertspoon chopped chives
¼ kg. (9 oz.) cream cheese   seasoning

Preparation
Nil.

Action

1. Mix the chives with the cream cheese and seasoning.
2. Place a teaspoon of the mixture in the centre of each slice of salami and pinch up the sides so that the salami forms a cross, then pull back two sides of the cross and fix them together with a blob of cream cheese. You should then have something which resembles a paper boat.

Not suitable for freezing.

Can be prepared a few hours in advance.

Hot

Cheese Sausage Rolls

335 g. (¾ lb.) cheese pastry   milk or egg for glazing
  (p. 197)
½ kg. (1 lb. 2 oz.) pork
  sausage meat

Preparation

Roll out the pastry into a long narrow strip, then cut into pieces approximately 6·25 cm. by 12·5 cm. (2½ in. by 5 in.). Roll the sausage meat into long narrow cartridge shapes.

Action

1. Put the sausage on the pastry. Dampen the edges and seal the long ends. Cut into rolls 2·5 cm.–5 cm. (1–2 in.) long.
2. Place the rolls on a baking sheet so that they do not touch. Glaze with a little milk or beaten egg. Cook in a hot oven for 10–15 minutes.

Suitable for freezing.

Can be prepared in advance.

Note: The sausage rolls can be made with shortcrust or flaky pastry if preferred.

35

Hot

Three Pizza Pies

For the Dough
170 g. (6 oz.) flour
10 g. ($\frac{1}{3}$ oz.) dried yeast
1 dl. ($\frac{1}{6}$ pint) warm water
pinch salt
3 dessertspoons oil for oiling
baking-tray

For the Basic Filling
60 g. (2 oz.) mozzarella or
bel paese cheese
60 g. (2 oz.) Gruyère cheese
$\frac{1}{4}$ kg. (9 oz.) tomatoes
$\frac{1}{2}$ teaspoon basil
seasoning

ALTERNATIVE ADDITIONS TO BASIC FILLING

(a) 4 anchovy fillets
(b) 110 g. (4 oz.) frozen
chopped spinach

(c) 110 g. (4 oz.) peeled
prawns

Preparation

Cut the cheese into thin strips. Peel and slice the tomatoes. Stone the olives if using (a), or defrost the spinach if using (b).

Action

1. Make the dough as follows: sift the flour into a basin with the salt. Mix the yeast with the warm water. Make a well in the flour, mix in the yeast and water to make an elastic dough and knead until well mixed. Put the dough in a warm place for 2 hours to rise.

2. When the dough has risen, turn it on to a floured board and knead again, then roll out to the thickness of 8 mm. ($\frac{1}{3}$ in.).

3. Well oil a baking-tray and spread the dough on top. Cover the dough with the tomatoes, basil and seasoning, and with whichever other filling you have chosen, then cover with the cheese.

4. Place in a hot oven for 20 minutes. Cut into fingers to serve.

Suitable for freezing.

Can be prepared in advance until 4.

Note: A commercial brand of pizza mix can be used for the dough, but it should be cooked for 20 minutes and not 15 as is often directed on the packets.

Hot

Stuffed Mushrooms

½ kg. (1 lb. 2 oz.) small
  mushrooms
220 g. (½ lb.) cottage cheese
2 tablespoons fresh white
  breadcrumbs

1 tablespoon oil
60 g. (2 oz.) butter
1 tablespoon chopped chives
seasoning

Preparation

Wash the mushrooms and remove stems.

Action

1. Mix the chives with the cottage cheese. Season.

2. Brush the outside of the mushrooms with the oil and fill with the cheese mixture. Sprinkle the breadcrumbs over the top and dot with butter.

3. Place in a hot oven for 10 minutes.

Not suitable for freezing.

Can be prepared in advance until 3.

Cold

Six Variations on a Stuffed Tomato
16 medium-sized tomatoes per recipe

Fillings

1. 450 g. (1 lb.) Philadelphia
     cheese
   ½ small green pepper
   ¼ teaspoon minced fresh
     basil
   pepper

2. 450 g. (1 lb.) Philadelphia
     cheese
   110 g. (¼ lb.) ham or bacon
   pepper

37

Fillings

3. 450 g. (1 lb.) Philadelphia
    cheese
    60 g. (2 oz.) bacon
    60 g. (2 oz.) peeled prawns
    pepper
4. 335 g. (¾ lb.) smoked
    buckling pâté (p. 23) or
    buy ready-made
    1 tablespoon lemon juice
    1 tablespoon mayonnaise

5. 220 g. (½ lb.) sardines
    6 anchovy fillets
6. 450 g. (1 lb.) Philadelphia
    cheese
    110 g. (¼ lb.) white crab-
    meat
    1 tablespoon tomato
    ketchup
    pepper

Preparation

For all the recipes, wash the tomatoes, cut the tops off, and scoop out the insides. Turn them upside down to drain while you prepare the fillings.

Action: Making the Fillings

1. Wash, deseed and mince the green pepper. Mash with the cheese and basil and add pepper to taste.
2. If using bacon, remove the rind, fry crisply in its own fat, then crumble. If using ham, chop finely. Mix either with the cheese. Season with pepper.
3. Crisply fry the bacon (remove the rind) in its own fat, then crumble. Cut the prawns into two or three pieces. Mix both bacon and prawns with the cheese and add pepper to taste.
4. Mix the buckling pâté with the lemon juice and mayonnaise.
5. Mash together the sardines and anchovy fillets, using a little of the oil from the sardines to moisten.
6. Extract any bone or sinews from the crabmeat. Mix it well with the cheese and tomato ketchup. Season to taste with pepper.

To Complete

For all the recipes, stuff the tomatoes with the mixture.

Not suitable for freezing.

Can be prepared a few hours in advance.

Note: We recommend you to use the size of tomatoes that can be eaten in not more than two mouthfuls, and not to skin them, since they are much easier to eat in the fingers when unpeeled. We suggest you dust them with a flurry of paprika before handing them round.

Cold

Avocado Balls

4 avocado pears	1 large packet potato crisps
½ onion	seasoning
1 lemon	

Preparation

Cut the avocados in half, remove the stones and scoop out the flesh. Peel the onion and finely grate it. Squeeze the juice from the lemon. Crush the crisps.

Action

1. Mash the avocados with the onion, lemon juice and seasoning.
2. Roll teaspoonfuls of the mixture in the crushed crisps.

Not suitable for freezing.

Can be prepared a few hours in advance. The crisps will stay crisp for about 5 hours.

Cold

Celery Cheese

2 heads celery	110 g. (¼ lb.) butter
220 g. (½ lb.) Danish blue cheese	seasoning

Preparation

Trim, wash and scrape the celery. Discard the narrow green tops to the sticks. Slice the celery into boats 2·5 cm. (1 in.) long.

Action

Season the celery boats. Fill first with butter and then with cheese.

Not suitable for freezing.

Can be prepared a few hours in advance.

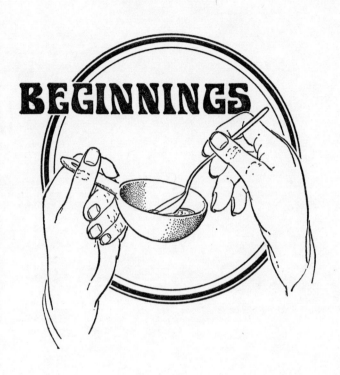

Cold

Pâté Eggs

220 g. (½ lb.) chicken liver
  pâté (p. 25)
12 eggs

6 dl. (1 pint) mayonnaise
  (p. 201)
seasoning

Preparation

Hard boil the eggs. Cool. Shell, slice in half lengthways and remove the yolks.

Action

1. Fill the egg whites with the pâté. Season.
2. Place the pâté-filled whites in a dish together with all but three of the hard-boiled yolks. Pour over the mayonnaise.
3. Very finely chop the remaining yolks and scatter over the top of the mayonnaise. Chill until required.

Not suitable for freezing.

Can be prepared in advance.

Cold

Lenten Eggs

6 eggs
2 large avocado pears
1 420 g. (15 oz.) tin palm
  hearts

6 dl. (1 pint) mayonnaise
  (p. 201)
seasoning

Preparation

Hard boil the eggs. Cool, shell and slice. Drain and chop the palm hearts. Cut the avocado pears in half, remove the stones, peel and slice.

Action

Arrange the egg carefully with the avocado and palm hearts in individual bowls. Season and pour over the mayonnaise.

Not suitable for freezing.

Not suitable for advance preparation.

Cold

Framed Eggs

6 eggs
½ kg. (1 lb. 2 oz.) courgettes
1 large cucumber
60 g. (2 oz.) butter

6 dl. (1 pint) mayonnaise
   (p. 201)
seasoning

Preparation

Wash and top and tail the courgettes, then cut each into four or five pieces. Peel and chop the cucumber.

Action

1. Put the courgettes in boiling salted water to cover, with the butter, and cook for 8 minutes. Drain and cool.

2. Hard boil the eggs. Cool, peel and slice.

3. Arrange the eggs with the courgettes and cucumber. Season. Pour the mayonnaise over the top.

Not suitable for freezing.

Not suitable for advance preparation.

Cold

Curried Prawn and Egg Mousse

110 g. (¼ lb.) peeled prawns
8 eggs
1 420 g. (15 oz.) tin
   consommé*
2 tablespoons salad cream

4 tablespoons double cream
1 tablespoon lemon juice
1 teaspoon curry powder
freshly ground black pepper

Preparation

Mix the curry powder with the cream. Hard boil the eggs. Peel, chop and cool.

Action

1. Place the eggs in a blender with the consommé and mix until smooth.
2. To the eggs and consommé, add the salad cream (not home-made mayonnaise on this occasion), cream and lemon juice to taste. Season with plenty of freshly ground black pepper.
3. Divide the prawns up between 8 ramekins, reserving 8 for decoration. Pour over the mousse, and chill in the refrigerator until required, but in any case for 3 hours to allow the consommé to set. Garnish with the reserved prawns, and possibly a little consommé or aspic.

Not suitable for freezing.

Can be prepared in advance.

*Note: Crosse & Blackwell consommé is much better for this recipe than any other, since it sets more firmly.

Hot

Cheese and Prawn Soufflé

140 g. (5 oz.) mild English cheese	85 g. (3 oz.) butter
110 g. (¼ lb.) peeled prawns	60 g. (2 oz.) flour
6 eggs	3 dl. (½ pint) milk
2 egg whites	seasoning

Preparation

Grate the cheese. Cut the prawns in half. Separate the eggs.

Action

1. Make a white sauce with the butter, flour and milk (p. 203). When the sauce has cooked for 4 minutes, stir in the grated cheese and continue stirring until the cheese has melted.
2. Cool slightly, then blend in the egg yolks and add the prawns. Season.
3. Whisk the egg whites until they are stiff, then blend half in, stirring well. Lightly fold in the other half.

45

4. Pour the mixture into 8 ramekin dishes and place in a moderate oven for 15 minutes.

Not suitable for freezing.

Not suitable for advance preparation.

Hot

Chicken and Prawn Soufflé

1 small half breast of chicken	85 g. (3 oz.) butter
110 g. (¼ lb.) peeled prawns	60 g. (2 oz.) flour
6 eggs	1½ dl. (¼ pint) milk
2 egg whites	seasoning

Preparation

Mince the prawns. Separate the eggs.

Action

1. Cover the chicken with water and simmer in a covered pan for 20 minutes. Cool.
2. Reserve 3 tablespoons of the resulting stock and remove the chicken from the bone, discarding the skin. Put the chicken and the juice in a blender or through a Mouli.
3. Make a thick white sauce with the butter, flour and milk (p. 203). When the sauce has cooked for 4 minutes, stir in the chicken purée and the minced prawns. Season, and cool.
4. When the mixture has cooled, blend in the egg yolks.
5. Whisk the egg whites until they are stiff, then blend half in, stirring well. Lightly fold in the other half.
6. Pour the mixture into 8 ramekin dishes and cook in a moderate oven for 15 minutes.

Not suitable for freezing.

Can be prepared in advance until 5.

Cold

Camembert Pots

½ kg. (1 lb. 2 oz.) Camembert
cheese
60 g. (2 oz.) fine fresh white
breadcrumbs

9 dl. (1½ pints) single cream
seasoning

Preparation

Scrape the rind from the cheeses and discard.

Action

1. Melt the cheese in a saucepan over a gentle heat.
2. Stir in the cream and seasoning. When everything is well stirred
   together, pour the mixture into 8 individual pots. Chill until
   required.
3. Place the breadcrumbs in the bottom of your grill pan and
   grill until they are brown, shaking the grill pan so that the
   crumbs remain separate and become brown evenly.
4. Sprinkle the crumbs on the cheese pots just before serving.

Suitable for freezing without the crumbs.

Can be prepared in advance.

Hot or cold

Armada Soup

2 420 g. (15 oz.) tins lobster
bisque
110 g. (¼ lb.) peeled prawns
1 large onion
4 cloves garlic
1 green pepper
1 aubergine
¼ kg. (9 oz.) courgettes

¼ kg. (9 oz.) tomatoes
4 tablespoons oil
1½ dl. (¼ pint) mild stock
(p. 198)
3 tablespoons sherry
½ teaspoon basil
seasoning

Preparation

Peel and chop the onion and garlic. Wash, deseed and finely chop the pepper. Wash, top and tail, and cube the aubergine. Wash, top and tail, and slice the courgettes. Skin and chop the tomatoes.

Action

1. Put the onion and garlic with the oil in a covered pan and cook over a moderate heat for 7 minutes.
2. Add the green pepper and cook for a further 5 minutes, taking care the vegetables don't burn.
3. Add the aubergine, courgettes and tomatoes. Sprinkle over the basil and season. Turn the heat lower and leave to cook gently for 50 minutes. Cool.
4. Mix with the stock and the lobster bisque and put into a blender, or a Mouli. Adjust the seasoning.
5. Stir in the sherry and the prawns and either chill or heat to simmering point, but do not boil.

Not suitable for freezing.

Can be prepared in advance.

Hot

Smoked Haddock Soup

¼ kg. (9 oz.) smoked haddock	6 dl. (1 pint) creamy milk
1 large onion	1½ dl. (¼ pint) double cream
2–3 tablespoons mashed potato	seasoning
60 g. (2 oz.) butter	2 tablespoons chopped parsley
9 dl. (1½ pints) water	for garnishing

Preparation

Wash the fish. Peel and chop the onion.

Action

1. Place the fish, onion and water in a saucepan and bring to the boil. Simmer for 7 minutes then extract the fish. Flake the fish

48

and return the skin and bones to the stock and continue to simmer for 30 minutes.

2. Strain the stock into a blender or Mouli. Add the mashed potato and haddock and mix until smooth.

3. Tip the contents of the blender into a saucepan with the milk and butter. Heat gently and season well. Just before serving, stir in the cream, but do not allow to boil. Serve garnished with parsley.

Suitable for freezing.

Can be prepared in advance.

Hot

Crab Bisque

220 g. ($\frac{1}{2}$ lb.) brown and white crabmeat	1$\frac{1}{2}$ dl. ($\frac{1}{4}$ pint) dry vermouth
1 large onion	4 dl. ($\frac{2}{3}$ pint) double cream
4 tomatoes	2 tablespoons brandy
9 dl. (1$\frac{1}{2}$ pints) water	$\frac{1}{2}$ teaspoon paprika
1 tablespoon oil	seasoning

Preparation

Peel and chop the onion. Skin the tomatoes and cut in quarters.

Action

1. In a large covered saucepan sauté the onion in the oil until soft (about 8 minutes). Add the water, crabmeat, tomatoes and paprika and simmer for 10 minutes.

2. Remove lid and increase heat. Continue cooking for a further 15 minutes, reducing the quantity by about a quarter.

3. Add the vermouth and adjust seasoning.

4. Stir in the cream, and heat but do not boil.

5. Add the brandy when the soup has been served.

Not suitable for freezing.

Can be prepared in advance.

Cold

Salmon Vichyssoise

¼ kg. (9 oz.) salmon, cut from   60 g. (2 oz.) butter
   the middle   1½ litres (2¼ pints) chicken
4 leeks   stock (p. 199)
4 potatoes   2 dl. (⅓ pint) double cream
1 stick celery   seasoning

Preparation

Thoroughly wash and trim the leeks, removing the dark green part, then slice the white part in half and leave to soak for at least 1 hour. Peel the potatoes and slice thinly. Trim, wash and scrape the celery and slice.

Action

1. Thinly slice the leeks, then put them in a saucepan with the butter and seasoning. Cover the pan and cook over a low heat for 10 minutes, or until the leeks are soft, taking care not to allow them to brown.
2. Add the potatoes, celery and stock. Season and simmer covered until all the vegetables are soft (about 20 minutes).
3. Tip the contents of the pan into a blender and mix until smooth, or rub through a sieve.
4. Put the salmon in a pan of fast boiling salted water. Cover and cook for 2 minutes. Remove the pan from the heat and allow the salmon to cool in the water.
5. When cool, drain. Remove the skin and backbone, then carefully flake the salmon. It divides naturally into spoon-size pieces; do not try to salvage small pieces from the skin or backbone as this will spoil the consistency of the soup.
6. Strain the soup into a bowl, then stir in the cream. Adjust seasoning. Pour into individual bowls and divide the salmon equally between them. Chill until required.

Not suitable for freezing.

Can be prepared in advance.

Cold

Calamari Yoghourt Soup

1½ litres (2½ pints) natural   1 tablespoon black caviare
  yoghourt   2 tablespoons chopped parsley
335 g. (¾ lb.) calamari (squid)   seasoning
170 g. (6 oz.) peeled prawns

Preparation

Remove the ink sacks, fins and skin from the calamari, turning
them inside out to remove the bone and jelly from inside. Reserve
the tentacles, which should be cut off just below the ink sacks.

Action

1. Simmer the calamari and tentacles with a little seasoning and
   sufficient water to cover in a closed pan for 15 minutes. Drain.
   Cool and chop into narrow strips.
2. Put the yoghourt into individual bowls. Add the calamari and
   prawns. Season and chill.
3. At the point of service, put equal quantities of caviare on each
   dish, taking care not to allow it to sink. Sprinkle over the
   chopped parsley.

Not suitable for freezing.

Can be prepared in advance until 3.

Cold

Smoked Yoghourt Soup

1½ litres (2½ pints) natural   ½ small cooked cauliflower
  yoghourt   seasoning
170 g. (6 oz.) smoked cod's
  roe

Preparation

Scrape the roe from the skin. Discard any hard pieces, which
  means you may have to throw away nearly half. (This has been
  allowed for.)

51

Action

Mix the cauliflower, smoked cod's roe and yoghourt in a blender or Mouli until smooth. Season and chill.

Not suitable for freezing.

Can be prepared a few hours in advance.

Cold

Anita's Yoghourt Soup

1½ litres (2½ pints) natural
   yoghourt
195 g. (7 oz.) peeled prawns
2 avocado pears
3 tablespoons chopped celery
1 dessertspoon finely chopped
   onion

1 dessertspoon tomato purée
½ teaspoon tabasco sauce
1 teaspoon paprika
3 tablespoons peanuts
seasoning

Preparation

Cut the avocado pears in half, remove the stones, peel and slice into small pieces.

Action

1. Stir the tomato purée and tabasco sauce into the yoghourt. Season.

2. Place equal portions of the prawns, avocado, celery and onion into individual bowls.

3. Pour the yoghourt into the bowls. Chill until you are ready to eat.

4. At the point of service stir in the peanuts (they will go soggy if you add them too early), and dust with a flurry of paprika.

Not suitable for freezing.

Can be prepared a few hours in advance until 4.

Cold
Yoghourt Curry Soup

1 litre (1¾ pints) natural   4 dl. (⅔ pint) jellied
  yoghourt   consommé (p. 55)
1 cucumber   seasoning
¾ teaspoon curry powder

Preparation
Peel and dice the cucumber.

Action
Mix the curry powder with the yoghourt. Season. Put the yoghourt
into individual bowls. Cover with the diced cucumber and the
jellied consommé. Keep in the refrigerator until required.
Not suitable for freezing.
Can be prepared in advance.

Hot
French Onion Soup

4 large onions   60 g. (2 oz.) butter
110 g. (¼ lb.) Gruyère cheese   1¾ litres (3 pints) water
8 slices French bread   seasoning

Preparation
Grate the cheese. Peel and thinly slice and chop the onions.

Action
1. Heat the butter in a large saucepan and fry the onions until
   brown, but not burnt.
2. Pour on the water and add salt and plenty of freshly ground
   black pepper. Cook for 45 minutes until the liquid has reduced
   by a quarter. Adjust the seasoning.
3. Pour the soup into individual ovenproof bowls. Float a slice
   of French bread on top of each and sprinkle the cheese evenly
   on top.

4. Place in a hot oven for 10 minutes to melt the cheese, then serve immediately.

Not suitable for freezing.

Can be prepared in advance until 3.

Hot

Vegetarian Soup

3 onions	1½ litres (2½ pints) water
450 g. (1 lb.) tomatoes	1 teaspoon vegetable extract
2 handfuls large macaroni	seasoning
60 g. (2 oz.) butter	

Preparation

Peel and chop the onions and peel and chop the tomatoes.

Action

1. Put the butter and onions into a covered pan and cook for 15 minutes, or until the onions are yellow to brown.
2. Add the water, tomatoes, vegetable extract and seasoning. Squeeze the handfuls of macaroni so that some of the pasta is broken, and add to the pan. Simmer for 30 minutes.

Suitable for freezing.

Can be prepared in advance.

Hot or cold

Lettuce Soup

2 cabbage lettuces	3 dl. (½ pint) single cream
2 onions	2 dl. (⅓ pint) commercially
60 g. (2 oz.) butter	soured cream
60 g. (2 oz.) flour	¼ nutmeg (grated)
1¼ litres (2 pints) strong	seasoning
chicken stock (p. 199)	

Preparation

Wash the lettuces and roughly shred. Peel and chop the onions.

Action

1. Heat the butter in a very large saucepan and cook the onions until soft but not brown.

2. Add the lettuce. Cover the pan and cook over a low heat for 10 minutes.

3. Add the stock, the grated nutmeg and seasoning and bring to the boil. Cover the pan and simmer gently for 20 minutes.

4. Whisk the flour into the cream, then mix into the soup. Bring to the boil and continue cooking, stirring constantly, until the soup thickens. Adjust seasoning.

5. Withdraw the pan from the heat and tip the contents into a blender or Mouli and mix until smooth.

6. Either return to the saucepan and heat, or chill until required. Serve with a blob of sour cream on each bowl.

Suitable for freezing.

Can be prepared in advance.

Hot or cold

Consommé

¾ kg. (1 lb. 11 oz.) minced shin of beef	1½ dl. (¼ pint) sherry
1 large uncooked chicken carcass with remains of meat	2 egg whites
	2 teaspoons salt
	1 bayleaf
	1 sprig parsley
110 g. (¼ lb.) onions	1 sprig thyme
110 g. (¼ lb.) carrots	6 peppercorns
1 stick celery	oil if necessary (see recipe)
2¼ litres (3¾ pints) water	

Preparation

Peel and thickly slice the onions and carrots. Trim, wash and scrape the celery. Make up a bouquet garni with the bayleaf, parsley and thyme and secure in a piece of muslin.

Action
1. Put the meat and bones in a large pan and brown evenly over a moderate heat, adding the onion half way through. (If the meat is exceptionally lean, you may have to add a little oil, but do not do so unless absolutely essential.)
2. Add the carrots, celery, bouquet garni, salt, peppercorns and water. Bring to the boil and simmer uncovered for 3–4 hours, or until the quantity has reduced to about 1¾ litres (3 pints).
3. Strain off and cool.
4. When the liquid has set to a jelly, remove the layer of fat which will probably have formed.*

To Clarify the Soup
5. Return the jelly to a saucepan and add the sherry.
6. Whisk the egg whites until frothy, then add to the pan and whisk in an anti-clockwise motion over a moderate heat.
7. When the soup reaches boiling point, stop whisking and allow the soup to boil up to the top of the pan. Withdraw the pan from the heat for a few minutes and let it subside.
8. Bring to the boil once more, taking care not to break the crust on top.
9. Boil a clean cloth and wring out, then pour the soup through it whilst holding back the crust with a spoon. When all the soup has gone through, slide the crust on to the cloth.
10. Pour the soup through the crust on the cloth once more and it should now be completely clear. Serve either hot or cold, jellied, with perhaps a little more sherry added, and a lemon wedge per person.

Not suitable for freezing if serving cold as it loses its clarity. This is not quite so important when serving hot.

Can be prepared in advance.

Notes: At this stage, you can boil the soup up again for 1 hour with the addition of a further ¾ kg. (1 lb. 11 oz.) minced shin, but this does make it excessively expensive, although you will get a richer soup.

This is a lengthy and expensive soup to make anyway, and for this reason it is best justified if you use the meat to make rissoles (p. 130). Obviously, much of the flavour will have gone from the meat so a particularly tasty binding sauce will be necessary.

Hot

Paupers' Soup

1 cooked chicken carcass
6 cloves garlic
½ kg. (1 lb. 2 oz.) potatoes

1 small green cabbage
1½ litres (2½ pints) water
seasoning

Preparation

Peel and chop the garlic. Peel and slice the potatoes. Wash and chop the cabbage.

Action

1. Remove any nice-looking pieces of chicken from the carcass and reserve. Crush the carcass and place in a muslin cloth. Simmer in the water for 1 hour.

2. Add the garlic, potatoes, cabbage and chicken pieces. Season and simmer for a further 30 minutes. Remove the muslin-wrapped chicken and discard. Adjust seasoning and serve.

Not suitable for freezing.

Can be prepared in advance.

Hot

Devilled Soft Roes

½ kg. (1 lb. 2 oz.) soft herring
  roes
85 g. (3 oz.) butter
2 tablespoons lemon juice
1 heaped teaspoon curry
  powder

⅛ teaspoon cayenne pepper
2 tablespoons seasoned flour
  (p. 198)

57

Preparation

Add the curry powder and cayenne pepper to the seasoned flour.
Coat the soft roes with it.

Action

1. Butter generously 8 individual ramekin dishes with about half
   the butter. Divide the roes evenly between them. Sprinkle over
   the lemon juice and dot with the rest of the butter.

2. Cook in a hot oven for 10 minutes.

Not suitable for freezing.

Not suitable for advance preparation.

Cold

Cottage Tuna

335 g. (¾ lb.) tuna fish   1 dessertspoon chopped chives
¼ kg. (9 oz.) cottage cheese   seasoning
3 sticks chicory
1–2 tablespoons French
  dressing (p. 202)

Preparation

Wash and slice the chicory.

Action

1. Mash the tuna fish in its oil with the cottage cheese and chives.
   Season and moisten with the French dressing. Mix in the
   chicory.

2. Pile on to individual plates and garnish with perhaps a little
   chopped parsley.

Not suitable for freezing.

Can be prepared in advance.

Cold

Haddock Mousse

½ kg. (1 lb. 2 oz.) smoked
  haddock
3 eggs
45 g. (1½ oz.) butter
45 g. (1½ oz.) flour

2 dl. (⅓ pint) milk
1½ dl. (¼ pint) double cream
1 dessertspoon gelatin
seasoning

Preparation

Wash and trim the haddock and soak for half an hour to remove
excess salt. Separate the eggs. Whip the cream. Soak the gelatin
with 2 tablespoons water.

Action

1. Place the haddock in a saucepan with the milk and some
   freshly ground black pepper. Bring to the boil and simmer for
   7 minutes. Strain the juice into a jug, and when the fish is
   sufficiently cool to handle carefully remove any skin and bones.

2. While the fish is cooling, make a thick white sauce with the
   butter, flour and fish juice (p. 203). When the sauce has boiled
   for 4 minutes, withdraw the pan from the heat and stir in the
   gelatin, making sure it dissolves completely.

3. Remove the pan from the heat and mix a little of the sauce
   with the egg yolk, then tip the egg yolks into the sauce. Make
   sure the sauce is not too hot, or it will scramble the egg.

4. Mash the fish as finely as possible and stir into the sauce,
   mixing until it is smooth. When it is smooth, stir in the whipped
   cream.

5. Whisk the egg whites until stiff and fold these in. Adjust the
   seasoning. Pour the mixture into individual ramekins, and
   put into the refrigerator to set until required (at least 3 hours).

Suitable for freezing.

Can be prepared in advance.

Cold

Smoked Salmon Velvet

3 eggs
3 dl. (½ pint) double cream
4 teaspoons smoked salmon
   mayonnaise

4½ dl. (¾ pint) aspic jelly
seasoning

Preparation

Separate the eggs.

Action

1. Make the aspic jelly following the directions on the packet and allow to cool.
2. Mix 1 teaspoon of the smoked salmon mayonnaise with the egg yolks and stir into the aspic. Whisk the egg whites and fold in. Stir in the cream.
3. Spoon into individual dishes and place in the refrigerator. When set, decorate with the remaining teaspoon of smoked salmon mayonnaise.

Not suitable for freezing.

Can be prepared in advance.

Cold

Chunky Salmon Pâté

560 g. (1¼ lb.) salmon
½ cucumber
140 g. (5 oz.) butter
4 dl. (⅔ pint) mild stock (p. 198)
5 tablespoons mayonnaise
   (p. 201)

1 dessertspoon lemon juice
1 bayleaf
seasoning

Preparation

Wash the salmon. Peel and dice the cucumber. Take the butter out of the refrigerator to soften.

Action

1. Put the salmon in the stock with the bayleaf and lemon juice. Bring to the boil and simmer for 2 minutes. Remove from the heat and, keeping covered, allow the salmon to cool completely in the stock.
2. When the salmon is cold, remove from the stock and separate the flesh from the skin and bones.
3. Put the salmon, butter and mayonnaise in a large bowl and mix together with your fingers. (This is better than using a fork which mashes the salmon. What you should be doing is integrating the salmon flakes with the butter and mayonnaise.)
4. Mix in the diced cucumber and seasoning. Transfer to 8 individual ramekins and chill until required.

Not suitable for freezing.

Can be prepared in advance.

Cold

Scampi Pâté

670 g. (1½ lb.) cooked scampi
170 g. (6 oz.) butter
3 tablespoons mayonnaise
   (p. 201)

1 dessertspoon chopped fresh
   chives
seasoning

Preparation

Peel the scampi and chop each into about three pieces. Take the butter out of the refrigerator to soften.

Action

1. Put the scampi in a large bowl and mix with the butter with your fingers.
2. Add the mayonnaise and continue to mix. Finally, add the chives. Adjust the seasoning and put into individual ramekins. chill until required.

Not suitable for freezing.

Can be prepared a few hours in advance.

Hot

Stuffed Artichoke Hearts

8 fresh or frozen globe
    artichoke hearts
¼ kg. (9 oz.) crabmeat
110 g. (¼ lb.) Gruyère cheese
30 g. (1 oz.) butter
30 g. (1 oz.) flour

3 dl. (½ pint) milk
seasoning
1 bayleaf, 1 dessertspoon oil
    and a few peppercorns if
    using fresh artichokes

Preparation

If using fresh artichokes, which are much better, cook them by boiling in salted water, to which should be added the bayleaf, oil and peppercorns, for about 45 minutes, or until the leaves pull out easily. If using frozen hearts, leave to defrost for 2 hours at room temperature. Remove any sinews from the crabmeat. Grate the cheese.

Action

1. Place the artichoke hearts in 8 individual ramekin dishes and cover each with one-eighth of the crabmeat.
2. With the butter, flour and milk, make a white sauce (p. 203). After the sauce has boiled for 4 minutes, withdraw the pan from the heat and stir in half the cheese. Season carefully.
3. Pour equal quantities of the sauce into each ramekin, and sprinkle over the rest of the cheese.
4. Cook in a hot oven for 12 minutes, crisping the top under the grill at the last moment if necessary.

Suitable for freezing before 4, if using fresh artichoke hearts and crabmeat.

Can be prepared in advance until 4.

Cold

Jackson's Avocado Folly

4 avocado pears
170 g. (6 oz.) peeled prawns
1 onion
4 tablespoons mayonnaise
  (p. 201)

½ teaspoon paprika
seasoning

Preparation

Peel and grate the onion. Slice the avocados in half lengthways
and remove the flesh, preserving the shells.

Action

Mash the avocados and season. Mix with the onion, prawns and
mayonnaise and return to the shells. Dust with paprika.

Not suitable for freezing.

Can be prepared up to 2 hours in advance.

Note: The avocados do not have to be perfectly ripe for this to be
good.

Cold

Prawn and Egg Mayonnaise

450 g. (1 lb.) large peeled
  prawns
4 eggs
1 small onion
2 dl. (⅓ pint) mayonnaise
  (p. 201)

1 tablespoon tomato purée
1 teaspoon curry powder
½ teaspoon oregano
seasoning

Preparation

Hard boil the eggs. Cool, shell and rough chop. Peel and grate or
mince the onion.

E   63

Action

1. Mix together the mayonnaise, onion, tomato purée, curry powder and oregano. Season to taste.
2. Add the eggs and prawns to the sauce and put in individual ramekins or glasses. Chill until required.

Not suitable for freezing.

Can be prepared in advance.

Cold

Crooner's Sea Food

450 g. (1 lb.) scallops   8 tablespoons mayonnaise
450 g. (1 lb.) calamari (squid)   (p. 201)
1 onion   1 dessertspoon lemon juice
1 lettuce   seasoning
3 tablespoons oil and vinegar
  dressing (p. 203)

Preparation

Clean the scallops. Remove the ink sacks, fins and skin from the calamari, turning them inside out to remove the bone and jelly from inside. Reserve the tentacles, which should be cut off just below the ink sacks, and put with the other calamari. Peel and slice the onion. Wash and shred the lettuce.

Action

1. Simmer the fish with sufficient water to cover, together with the onion and lemon juice, for 15 minutes.
2. Drain the fish, discarding the onion. Cut the scallops in half while still warm, and slice the calamari into strips. Mix with the oil and vinegar dressing. Season, and leave until required in the refrigerator.
3. To serve, place the lettuce in individual bowls or glasses, spoon the fish on top, and finally coat with the mayonnaise.

Not suitable for freezing.

Can be prepared a few hours in advance until 3.

Cold

Avocado and Prawn Mousse

4 avocado pears	1½ dl. (¼ pint) natural yoghourt
110 g. (¼ lb.) peeled prawns	1 tablespoon lemon juice
220 g. (½ lb.) Philadelphia	5 drops tabasco sauce
cheese	seasoning
½ small onion	

Preparation

Peel and very very finely chop or grate the onion. If time permits, mix this with the cheese and leave overnight for the flavours to blend.

Action

1. Mix together well the cheese, onion, yoghourt, lemon juice and tabasco sauce. Leave to stand for at least 3 hours.
2. Peel and stone the avocado pears and mash them with the cheese. Season carefully.
3. Stir in the prawns. Seal the bowl in a polythene bag to stop the avocados discolouring, until you are ready to serve, then serve on individual plates, possibly on a lettuce leaf, and dusted with a flurry of paprika.

Not suitable for freezing.

Can be prepared a few hours in advance (see 3).

Cold

Saracen Crab

½ kg. (1 lb. 2 oz.) crabmeat	4 dl. (⅔ pint) commercially
2 large avocado pears	soured cream
1 small honeydew melon	seasoning
½ lettuce	

Preparation

Wash and shred the lettuce. Slice the melon lengthways into eight pieces, then peel and remove the pips. Slice the avocados in half,

65

removing the stones, then cut lengthways in half again and peel the quarters.

Action

1. Place a crescent of avocado and one of melon on each plate so that together they form a ring.
2. Fill the hollow with shredded lettuce and then lay the crabmeat on top. Season lightly. Top with a large dollop of sour cream.

Not suitable for freezing.

Not suitable for advance preparation.

Hot

Spareribs

1 kg. (2¼ lb.) pork spareribs

For the Marinade

¼ kg. (9 oz.) tomatoes	2 tablespoons brown sugar
3 tablespoons tomato purée	¼ teaspoon chilli powder
1 slice lemon	¼ teaspoon celery salt
1 finely chopped onion	¼ teaspoon dry mustard
1 clove garlic	seasoning
2 tablespoons wine vinegar	
1 dessertspoon Worcester sauce	

Preparation

Trim any excess fat from the spareribs. Peel and purée the tomatoes. Peel and finely chop the onion and garlic.

Action

1. Mix all the marinade ingredients together in a large shallow dish. Put the spareribs in with it and see that they are well coated. Allow to marinate for at least 6 hours, turning the spareribs from time to time.
2. Grill, or preferably barbecue, the ribs until crisp, brushing frequently with the marinade as you do so.

66

Suitable for freezing before cooking.

Can be prepared in advance.

Note: Veal or lamb spareribs may also be used for this recipe.

Hot

Tripe and Mash

¾ kg. (1 lb. 11 oz.) tripe	4 dl. (⅔ pint) milk
2 onions	1 dl. (⅙ pint) sherry
170 g. (6 oz.) mushrooms	1 dessertspoon lemon juice
2 tablespoons oil	1 bayleaf
60 g. (2 oz.) butter	seasoning
45 g. (1½ oz.) flour	6 potatoes for mashing

Preparation

Wash the tripe, removing any fat. Peel and chop the onions. Wash and chop the mushrooms. Peel the potatoes.

Action

1. Boil the tripe in sufficient water to cover for 10 minutes.
2. Discard the water, and when the tripe is cool enough cut into thick matchsticks. Place the tripe in a saucepan with sufficient fresh water to cover, together with the onions, lemon juice, bayleaf and seasoning, and cook covered over a very moderate heat for 2 hours.
3. Sauté the mushrooms in the oil. Boil the potatoes in the ordinary way and mash.
4. Drain the water from the tripe, discarding the bayleaf.
5. With the butter, flour and milk, make a white sauce (p. 203). When the sauce has boiled for 4 minutes, add the sherry, the mushrooms and the tripe and onions. Season well. Serve surrounded by mashed potato in scallop shells or similar individual dishes. Warm in the oven before serving.

Suitable for freezing.

Can be prepared in advance.

Hot or cold

Onion Flan

2 large onions
4 eggs
60 g. (2 oz.) butter
3 dl. (½ pint) double cream

¼ nutmeg
seasoning
¼ kg. (9 oz.) shortcrust pastry
(p. 195)

Preparation
Peel and chop the onions.

Action

1. Roll out pastry to line a 23–25 cm. (9–10 in.) flan case. Bake blind in a hot oven for 10 minutes (p. 195).
2. Blanch the onions in boiling water for 5 minutes. Drain.
3. Heat the butter in a saucepan and sauté the onions until soft, but not brown.
4. When the flan case has cooked for 10 minutes, spread the onions over the bottom. Mix together the eggs, cream and seasoning and pour over the top. Grate the nutmeg over it.
5. Bake in a very moderate oven for about 40 minutes, or until the mixture has set.

Suitable for freezing.

Can be prepared in advance.

Hot

Leek and Anchovy Flan

4 medium leeks
60 g. (2 oz.) anchovies
110 g. (¼ lb.) Gruyère cheese
¼ kg. (9 oz.) tomatoes
85 g. (3 oz.) butter

1 heaped tablespoon flour
4 dl. (⅔ pint) milk
seasoning
1 kg. (9 oz.) shortcrust pastry
(p. 195)

Preparation

Thoroughly wash and trim the leeks, remove the dark green part and slice the white part. Chop all but three of the anchovies. These three you should split in half to use for garnish. Grate the cheese. Skin and chop the tomatoes.

Action

1. Roll out pastry to line a 23–25 cm. (9–10 in) flan case. Bake blind in a hot oven for 10 minutes (p. 195).

2. Heat the butter in a saucepan and add the leeks, stirring until the juice begins to come out, then cover and simmer gently for 20 minutes.

3. Sprinkle over the flour and cook, stirring constantly for 3 minutes, then blend in the milk. Bring to the boil, stirring constantly, then simmer for 4 minutes.

4. Remove the pan from the heat and stir in the cheese, tomatoes and chopped anchovies. Season very carefully, remembering that the cheese and anchovies will add quite a lot of saltiness. Cool the mixture.

5. When the mixture is cold, spread it over the bottom of the flan case and decorate with the remaining strips of anchovy. Bake in a moderately hot oven for 40 minutes.

Suitable for freezing, preferably before baking.

Can be prepared in advance.

Hot

Kipper Flan

335 g. (¾ lb.) kipper fillets	¼ teaspoon curry powder
12 capers	1 tablespoon chopped parsley
60 g. (2 oz.) butter	seasoning
60 g. (2 oz.) flour	¼ kg. (9 oz.) shortcrust pastry
6 dl. (1 pint) milk	(p. 195)
¼ teaspoon lemon pepper	

Preparation

Skin the kipper fillets and cut into pieces, removing any bones. Chop the capers.

Action

1. Roll out pastry to line a 23–25 cm. (9–10 in.) flan case. Bake blind in a hot oven for 10 minutes (p. 195).
2. Meanwhile make a white sauce with the butter, flour and milk (p. 203). When it has boiled for 4 minutes, withdraw the pan from the heat and stir in all the other ingredients. Add the lemon pepper and other seasoning and cool.
3. When the mixture is cold spread it in the pastry case.
4. Cook in a moderately hot oven for 40 minutes.

Suitable for freezing, preferably before baking.

Can be prepared in advance.

Hot

Marrakesh Aubergines

4 aubergines	110 g. (¼ lb.) tomato purée
8 cloves garlic	1 dl. (⅙ pint) chicken stock
2 tablespoons Parmesan cheese	(p. 199)
2 tablespoons currants	30 g. (1 oz.) butter
6 tablespoons oil	seasoning

Preparation

Wash, top and tail, and slice the aubergines. Peel and chop the garlic.

Action

1. Fry the aubergines in the oil until brown, then place in a shallow fire-proof dish, mixing with the currants, garlic and seasoning.
2. Dilute the tomato purée with the chicken stock and pour over the aubergines.

3. Sprinkle the Parmesan cheese over the top, dot with the butter and put in a moderately hot oven for 40 minutes.

Suitable for freezing.

Can be prepared in advance.

Hot or cold

Ratatouille

3 onions	1 kg. (2¼ lb.) tomatoes
3 cloves garlic	6 tablespoons oil
3 aubergines	1 teaspoon basil
3 green peppers	seasoning
6 courgettes	

Preparation

Peel and coarsely chop the onions and tomatoes. Wash, top and tail, and coarsely chop the aubergines and courgettes. Wash, deseed and chop the green peppers. Peel and chop the garlic.

Action

1. Heat the oil in a heavy saucepan and simmer the onions and garlic for 7 minutes.

2. Add the aubergines and green peppers to the pan. Cover and cook for 10 minutes, stirring occasionally.

3. Add the courgettes to the pan, cover again and continue cooking for 15 minutes.

4. Add the tomatoes, basil and seasoning. Cover and cook for another 30 minutes. Stir occasionally to make sure the vegetables aren't sticking.

5. Transfer to a serving dish if you are going to eat it hot, or cool and chill in the refrigerator until required.

Suitable for freezing.

Can be prepared in advance.

Cold

Avocado and Grapefruit Salad

2 avocado pears   1½ dl. (¼ pint) oil and vinegar
1 large grapefruit   dressing (p. 203)
2 lettuces   seasoning
2 tablespoons sultanas
2 tablespoons chopped
   almonds

Preparation

Peel the grapefruit, cutting deep through the white pith. Cut each
segment of fruit from the inner skins. Wash the lettuces.

Action

1. Add the sultanas and grapefruit to the lettuce leaves. Toss in the
   oil and vinegar dressing.
2. Cut the avocados in half, remove the stone and peel. Cut into
   thin slices and place on the salad. Don't toss with the avocado
   as this will make the salad mushy.
3. At the point of service, sprinkle over the nuts.

Not suitable for freezing.

Not suitable for advance preparation.

Cold

Spinach and Lettuce Salad

1 lettuce   1 green pepper
220 g. (½ lb.) fresh spinach   1½ dl. (¼ pint) French
2 red peppers   dressing (p. 202)

Preparation

Wash the lettuce and spinach leaves, discarding any that are
coarse or discoloured, and extracting the stalks from the spinach.
Wash, deseed and slice the peppers.

Action

Toss all the ingredients together in the French dressing.

Not suitable for freezing.

Not suitable for advance preparation.

Cold

Cucumber Mousse

1 large but young cucumber	3 dl. (½ pint) commercially
670 g. (1½ lb.) Philadelphia	soured cream
cheese	freshly ground black pepper
1 small onion	

Preparation

Peel and small dice the cucumber. Sprinkle with salt and leave tied in a piece of muslin, hanging over a bowl, to drip for 1 hour. Peel and grate the onion very finely.

Action

Mash together with a fork the cheese, onion and soured cream. Stir in the drained cucumber and season with plenty of freshly ground black pepper. Chill for at least 6 hours so that the onion flavour is absorbed, and keep in the refrigerator until required.

Not suitable for freezing.

Can be prepared in advance.

MAINS

Hot

Egg and Tomato Crumble

16 eggs
4 onions
¾ kg. (1 lb. 11 oz.) tomatoes
110 g. (¼ lb.) strong English
   cheese

8 tablespoons fresh white
   breadcrumbs
85 g. (3 oz.) butter
2 dessertspoons castor sugar
seasoning

Preparation

Grate the cheese. Peel and slice the onions and tomatoes.

Action

1. Hard boil the eggs. Peel and slice.
2. Sauté the onions in two-thirds of the butter for 10 minutes, or until soft, taking care not to allow them to brown.
3. Butter a heat-proof dish and put in it layers of onion, egg and tomato, seasoning each layer with salt and pepper, and the tomato layers with the sugar as well. Continue until all the ingredients are used up.
4. Mix together the grated cheese and breadcrumbs and sprinkle over the dish. Dot with the rest of the butter.
5. Bake in a moderately hot oven for 30 minutes, browning the top under the grill if necessary.

Not suitable for freezing.

Can be prepared in advance until 5.

Hot

Finnan Eggs

1 kg. (2¼ lb.) smoked haddock
8 eggs
140 g. (5 oz.) butter
85 g. (3 oz.) flour

7½ dl. (1¼ pints) milk
1½ dl. (¼ pint) double cream
seasoning
chopped parsley for garnishing

Preparation

Wash the fish.

77

Action

1. Poach the fish for 10 minutes with half the milk, 30 g. (1 oz.) of the butter, and some black pepper. At the same time put on the eggs to hard boil. When they are cooked, shell them and cut each into about 8 pieces.

2. When the fish is cooked, strain the juice into a jug and fillet the fish, carefully removing any bones or skin.

3. Make a white sauce with another 75 g. (2½ oz.) of the butter, the flour, fish stock and the rest of the milk (p. 203). Season carefully, remembering that the fish may be a little salt.

4. Remove the pan from the heat, stir in the cream and the rest of the butter. Add the fish and eggs to the sauce and tip into a casserole.

5. Heat very gently in a slow oven for 20 minutes. Adjust the seasoning and serve garnished with chopped parsley.

Not suitable for freezing.

Can be prepared in advance until 5.

Hot

Fish Pie

½ kg. (1 lb. 11 oz.) cod fillet	85 g. (3 oz.) butter
6 rashers back bacon	60 g. (2 oz.) flour
110 g. (¼ lb.) mild English cheese	4½ dl. (¾ pint) milk
4 leeks	1 tablespoon lemon juice
110 g. (¼ lb.) mushrooms	seasoning
6 tomatoes	about 6 potatoes for topping

Preparation

Cut the rind from the bacon and dice the meat. Grate the cheese. Thoroughly wash and trim the leeks, remove the dark green part, and slice the white parts. Peel the potatoes. Wash and slice the mushrooms. Peel and chop the tomatoes.

Action

1. Put the potatoes on to boil with some salt, and when cooked mash in the ordinary way.

2. Heat two-thirds of the butter in a frying-pan and sauté the bacon, leeks and mushrooms, sprinkled with the lemon juice and seasoning, for 15 minutes, stirring occasionally.

3. At the same time place the fish in a saucepan with the milk and a little pepper. Bring to the boil, then simmer for 7 minutes. Strain off the liquid into a jug and remove any bones and skin from the fish, then flake.

4. Heat the rest of the butter in a saucepan and with the flour, and the milk in which the fish was cooked, make a white sauce (p. 203). When the sauce has boiled for 4 minutes, withdraw the pan from the heat and stir in the cheese. When this has melted, stir in the contents of the frying-pan, the fish and the tomatoes. Season.

5. Place the fish in a large shallow heat-proof dish and pipe or spread the mashed potatoes round the edge.

6. Heat in a very moderate oven for 35 minutes.

Suitable for freezing before stage 6.

Can be prepared in advance until 6.

Hot

Visionary Fish

450 g. (1 lb.) cod fillet	1 orange
335 g. (¾ lb.) calamari (squid)	9 dl. (1½ pints) water
220 g. (½ lb.) scallops	1 tablespoon tarragon vinegar
3 onions	½ teaspoon poppy seeds
560 g. (1¼ lb.) potatoes	seasoning
½ lemon	

Preparation

Remove the ink sacks, fins and skin from the calamari, turning them inside out to remove the bone and jelly from inside. Reserve

F   79

the tentacles, which should be cut off just below the ink sacks, and put with the rest of the calamari. Clean the scallops. Peel and chop the onions. Peel and slice the potatoes. Squeeze the orange.

Action

1. Put everything except the potatoes, orange juice and scallops into a large saucepan and simmer for 15 minutes.
2. Remove the fish. Cut the calamari into three or four pieces. Discard the skin from the cod, and search for any bones.
3. Return the fish to the pan, discard the half lemon, and add the potatoes, scallops and orange juice. Bring to the boil, then simmer for 15 minutes. Adjust seasoning and serve.

Not suitable for freezing.

Can be prepared in advance until 3.

Hot

Octopus Stew

1¾ kg. (4 lb.) octopus	2 dl. (⅓ pint) water
450 g. (1 lb.) button onions	1 dl. (⅙ pint) sherry
140 g. (5 oz.) shelled peas	1 bayleaf
3 lettuce leaves	seasoning
60 g. (2 oz.) butter	

Preparation

Peel the onions. Wash the lettuce leaves.

Action

1. Place the octopus in a saucepan with the bayleaf, seasoning and sufficient water to cover. Cover and simmer for 1 hour. Cool in the water, then drain.
2. In another saucepan put the 2 dl. (⅓ pint) water, and add the onions, peas, lettuce leaves, butter and seasoning. Cover and cook for 20 minutes.
3. When the octopus is cold, cut into small pieces and add to the

vegetables. Add the sherry, adjust the seasoning and cook slowly in the covered pan for another 2 hours. Remove the lettuce leaves, and adjust seasoning before serving.

Suitable for freezing.

Can be prepared in advance.

Hot

Tuna Fish Casserole

¾ kg. (1 lb. 11 oz.) tuna fish	4 tablespoons fresh white
1 small head celery	breadcrumbs
1 red or green pepper	85 g. (3 oz.) butter
2 onions	60 g. (2 oz.) flour
170 g. (6 oz.) button mush-	6 dl. (1 pint) milk
rooms	2 tablespoons lemon juice
¼ kg. (9 oz.) noodles	seasoning

Preparation

Trim, wash, scrape and slice the celery. Wash, deseed and chop the pepper. Peel and chop the onions. Wash and slice the mushrooms.

Action

1. Heat 60 g. (2 oz.) of the butter in a heavy saucepan and sauté the vegetables, sprinkled with the lemon juice and plenty of seasoning, for 10 minutes.

2. Sprinkle the flour over the vegetables and cook, stirring constantly for 2 minutes, then blend in the milk and bring to the boil, continuing to stir. When the mixture has come to the boil, reduce the heat, cover the pan and simmer for 10 minutes. Adjust the seasoning.

3. Meanwhile, put on a pan of salted water to boil, and cook the noodles in this for 7–10 minutes, until soft. Drain.

4. Lightly butter a soufflé or casserole dish, and put a layer of noodles in the bottom, followed by a layer of tuna and a layer of vegetable sauce. Repeat this process until all the ingredients are used up.

5. Sprinkle over the breadcrumbs and dot with the remaining 30 g. (1 oz.) butter. Bake uncovered in a moderate oven for 35 minutes.

Not suitable for freezing.

Can be prepared in advance until 5.

Hot

Smoked Cod Casserole

900 g. (2 lb.) smoked cod fillets	85 g. (3 oz.) butter
6 leeks	2 tablespoons lemon juice
1 green pepper	¼ teaspoon thyme
1 small head celery	1 tablespoon chopped parsley
¼ kg. (9 oz.) tomatoes	seasoning

Preparation

Cut the fish into bite-size pieces and remove any stray bones. Thoroughly wash and trim the leeks, removing the dark green part, and slice the white parts. Trim, wash, scrape and slice the celery. Wash, deseed and chop the pepper. Peel and chop the tomatoes.

Action

1. Heat 60 g. (2 oz.) of the butter in a frying-pan and sauté the leeks, pepper and celery for 15 minutes, taking care not to allow them to brown. Stir in the tomatoes and sprinkle with the thyme and seasoning.

2. Transfer the contents of the pan to a casserole and lay the fish on top of the vegetables. Sprinkle with the lemon juice, parsley and pepper, and dot with the remaining 30 g. (1 oz.) butter. Cover, and cook in a very moderate oven for 40 minutes.

Suitable for freezing before the oven stage, providing the fish has not already been frozen.

Can be prepared in advance until the final cooking.

Hot

Kedgeree

670 g. (1½ lb.) smoked   8 tablespoons long grain rice
  haddock   ¼ kg. (9 oz.) butter
8 rashers bacon   seasoning
4 eggs   3 tablespoons chopped parsley
170 g. (6 oz.) button mush-   for garnishing
  rooms

Preparation

Trim the haddock and wash. Cut the rind from the bacon. Wash
and slice the mushrooms.

Action

1. Simmer the haddock in enough water to cover for 10 minutes.
2. At the same time, boil the rice in a large pan of fast-boiling
   salted water for 13 minutes. When cooked tip the rice into a
   sieve and run boiling water through it to separate the grains,
   then drain it thoroughly.
3. At the same time, hard boil the eggs, and when cooked peel
   and chop.
4. Fry the bacon in its own fat until crisp, then break into small
   pieces. Sauté the mushrooms in the resulting fat.
5. When the fish has cooked, allow it to cool slightly for easier
   handling, then extract the bones and skin and flake the fish.
6. Melt the butter in a large saucepan, and put in all the ingredients, except the parsley, and warm thoroughly, stirring all the
   time, so that nothing sticks. Season well.
7. Turn on to a large serving dish and garnish with the chopped
   parsley.

Not suitable for freezing.

Can be prepared in advance until 6.

Note: May be heated in a casserole in the oven if more convenient.

Cold

Cold Salmon Kedgeree

¾ kg. (1 lb. 11 oz.) cold cooked salmon
4 eggs
1 tablespoon grated onion
2 dessertspoons capers
8 tablespoons long grain rice

8 tablespoons mayonnaise (p. 201)
1½ dl. (¼ pint) single cream
3–4 tablespoons lemon juice
seasoning

Preparation

Flake the salmon, removing any skin and bones. Chop the capers.

Action

1. Cook the rice for 13 minutes in a pan of fast-boiling salted water. Drain and run under the cold tap in a sieve to cool. Drain again thoroughly.
2. Meanwhile hard boil the eggs. Shell, chop and cool.
3. In a large bowl, mix together the salmon, eggs, onion, capers and rice. Bind together with the mayonnaise and cream. Season with the lemon juice, salt and pepper if necessary.
4. Pile on to a serving plate and garnish with perhaps slices of lemon and parsley.

Not suitable for freezing.

Can be prepared in advance.

Cold

Salmon Mousse

¾ kg. (1 lb. 11 oz.) salmon
4 eggs
110 g. (¼ lb.) butter
110 g. (¼ lb.) flour
3 dl. (½ pint) milk
4½ dl. (¾ pint) water
1½ dl. (¼ pint) red wine
1 420 g. (15 oz.) tin consommé

3 dl. (½ pint) double cream
2 tablespoons lemon juice
1 tablespoon gelatin
1 bayleaf
sprig of parsley
seasoning

Preparation
Separate the eggs.

Action

1. Place the salmon in a saucepan with the water, one-third of the wine, the parsley, bayleaf and seasoning. Cover and bring to the boil. Cook for 5 minutes, remove from heat and allow to cool in the liquid.

2. Heat the consommé and dissolve the gelatin in it. Pour 2 dl. ($\frac{1}{3}$ pint) of it into a separate dish and reserve for use later as a glaze.

3. Make a white sauce with the butter, flour, milk, 1$\frac{1}{2}$ dl. ($\frac{1}{4}$ pint) of the fish liquid, and the remaining consommé (p. 203). Boil for 4 minutes.

4. Remove the pan from the heat and mix a little of the sauce with the egg yolks, then tip the egg yolks into the sauce, together with the rest of the wine and seasoning. Make sure the sauce is not too hot or it will scramble the egg. Mix well and leave to cool.

5. When the salmon is cool, take off the skin, carefully remove any bones, and flake the fish into the sauce. Place in a blender or Mouli and mix until smooth. Stir in the lemon juice.

6. Stir the cream into the mixture. Stiffly beat the egg whites and fold in. Adjust the seasoning. Pour into a soufflé dish and leave to set in the refrigerator.

7. When the mousse has set, garnish with perhaps sprigs of parsley and curls of lemon, or as you like. Spoon over the reserved consommé. It will probably be necessary to heat it again slightly, then cool it to get the right consistency, which is the moment it is *just* beginning to set.

Suitable for freezing.

Can be prepared in advance.

Cold

Curried Haddock

1 kg. (2¼ lb.) smoked haddock
   fillets
60 g. (2 oz.) butter
60 g. (2 oz.) flour
4½ dl. (¾ pint) milk
2 egg yolks
3 dl. (½ pint) double cream

1 heaped teaspoon curry
   powder
seasoning
¼ cucumber, 3–4 tomatoes and
   chopped parsley for
   garnishing

Preparation

Wash the haddock.

Action

1. Place the fish in a saucepan with the milk and some black
   pepper. Bring to the boil and simmer with the lid on the pan
   for 10 minutes. Strain the milk into a jug and reserve. Skin the
   fish and remove any bones. Flake the fish and place in a mixing
   bowl.

2. Make a white sauce with the butter, flour and reserved milk
   (p. 203). Bring to the boil and simmer for 4 minutes. Blend in
   the curry powder and cook for another 2 minutes. Withdraw
   the pan from the heat and cool slightly.

3. Remove the pan from the heat and mix a little of the sauce
   with the egg yolks, then tip back into the main sauce and mix
   until smooth. Make sure it is not too hot, or it will scramble
   the eggs. Season lightly, remembering that the haddock may be
   a bit salt.

4. Leave to cool, then mix in the cream. Pour over the fish and
   mix well.

5. Pile the fish onto a plate and garnish with alternate peeled
   slices of cucumber and tomatoes, and dust with finely chopped
   parsley. Chill until required.

Not suitable for freezing.

Can be prepared a few hours in advance.

Cold

Prawns in Aspic

670 g. (1½ lb.) large peeled   450 g. (1 lb.) tomatoes
  prawns   9 dl. (1½ pints) aspic jelly
1 small onion   2 tablespoons lemon juice
2 large ripe avocado pears   seasoning

Preparation

Peel and grate the onion very finely. Peel and slice the tomatoes
and deseed.

Action

1. Make up the aspic, following the directions on the packet.
   Cool as quickly as possible by putting in a shallow bowl
   surrounded by ice. Stir in the onion and lemon juice.

2. When the aspic is beginning to set, pour a little into a soufflé
   dish or similar. Skin the avocado pears, then slice. Put layers
   of prawns, avocados and tomatoes, seasoning each, between
   layers of aspic (waiting each time until the layer of aspic has
   set), until all is used up. This is a bit of a long process, which
   can be greatly speeded up if you have a freezer. When you have
   put in your first layer of prawns, pour over another layer of
   aspic, and set this in the deep freeze for about 5 minutes,
   then add the next ingredient and set the next layer of aspic in
   a similar way, continuing until all the ingredients are used up,
   and finishing with an aspic layer. Chill in the refrigerator for
   several hours.

3. At the point of service, turn the mould out on to a bed of lettuce
   (p. 199).

Not suitable for freezing.

Can be prepared in advance until 3.

Cold

Racing Scampi

1¼ kg. (2¾ lb.) frozen scampi
   tails in shells or approx. 16
   crawfish tails in their shells*
1 small onion
2 dl. (⅓ pint) white wine
4 tablespoons tomato purée
4½ dl. (¾ pint) commercially
   soured cream

4 drops tabasco sauce
¼ teaspoon thyme
¼ teaspoon oregano
½ teaspoon lemon pepper
   seasoning
rice
parsley and paprika for
   garnishing

Preparation

Defrost the scampi (3–4 hours at room temperature). Peel and very very finely chop or grate the onion. (Much the easiest way of doing this is to put it through a Mouli parsley chopper.)

Action

1. When the scampi are defrosted, put the onion, wine, herbs and lemon pepper into a saucepan. Cover and simmer gently for 7 minutes. At the same time put on a pan of salted water to boil for the rice, and when it is boiling, add the rice and cook for 13 minutes.
2. Add the scampi tails to the onion etc., and cook for 7 minutes.
3. Remove the scampi and leave to cool. Meanwhile withdraw the pan from the heat and stir in the tomato purée and tabasco sauce.
4. Shell the scampi and return them to the sauce, and when cold, stir in the soured cream and adjust the seasoning.
5. When the rice is cooked, pour into a sieve and run under the cold tap, then drain well.
6. Chill the rice and scampi until required, then make a circle with the rice, put the scampi in the middle and garnish with parsley and a flurry of paprika.

Not suitable for freezing.

Can be prepared a few hours in advance until 6.

**Note:* If using crawfish tails rather than scampi, cut them into bite-size pieces.

Hot

Tarragon Scampi

1¼ kg. (2¾ lb.) frozen scampi
    tails in shells or approx. 16
    crawfish tails in shells*
½ small onion
2 dl. (⅓ pint) white wine
4½ dl. (¾ pint) double cream

5 drops tabasco sauce
1 sprig fresh tarragon or ¼
    teaspoon dried tarragon
½ teaspoon lemon pepper
    seasoning

Preparation

Defrost the scampi (3–4 hours at room temperature). Peel and
very very finely chop or grate the onion. (Much the easiest way of
doing this is to put it through a Mouli parsley chopper.)

Action

1. When the scampi are defrosted, put the onion, wine, tabasco
   sauce, tarragon and lemon pepper into a saucepan. Cover and
   simmer gently for 7 minutes.

2. Add the scampi tails to the pan and cook for 7 minutes.

3. Remove the tarragon if using the fresh, which is best, and the
   scampi and leave to cool sufficiently to handle. Reduce the
   liquid, if necessary, by continuing to boil it until you are left
   with only 1½ dl. (¼ pint). Shell the scampi and return them to
   the pan.

4. When you are ready to eat, reheat the scampi very gently in
   the juice, and stir in the cream, taking care not to allow it to
   boil.

Not suitable for freezing.

Can be prepared a few hours in advance until 4.

*_Notes:_ If you are using crawfish tails rather than scampi, cut
them into bite-size pieces.

    This dish is best served with rice.

Hot

Jambalaya

½ kg. (1 lb. 2 oz.) ham
½ kg. (1 lb. 2 oz.) peeled
  prawns
3 onions
1 green pepper
1 clove garlic
¼ kg. (9 oz.) tomatoes
8 tablespoons rice

3 tablespoons oil
¾ litre (1¼ pints) chicken
  stock (p. 199)
8–10 drops tabasco sauce
2 bayleaves
1 heaped tablespoon chopped
  parsley
seasoning

Preparation

Cut the ham into thin strips. Wash, deseed and chop the green
pepper. Peel and slice the onions and tomatoes. Peel and finely
chop or squeeze the garlic.

Action

1. Heat the oil in a heavy pan and brown the ham, onions,
   peppers and garlic, stirring regularly until the vegetables are soft.
2. Add the tomatoes, rice, stock, tabasco sauce, bayleaves and
   plenty of seasoning, remembering that the rice will need quite
   a bit of salt. Bring to the boil. Cover the pan and cook for
   20 minutes over a moderate heat, stirring occasionally.
3. Stir in the prawns and cook for a further 5 minutes. Adjust
   seasoning.
4. Turn into a heated bowl and sprinkle over the chopped parsley.

Not suitable for freezing.

Can be prepared 30 minutes in advance and kept warm.

Hot

Breaded Scallops

1 kg. (2¼ lb.) small scallops
110 g. (¼ lb.) fresh white
  breadcrumbs
60 g. (2 oz.) butter

1½ dl. (¼ pint) white wine
¼ teaspoon lemon balm or
  lemon thyme
seasoning

Preparation

Mix the herbs with the breadcrumbs. If necessary, take the scallops from their shells, but frozen ones are quite adequate.

Action

1. Spread half the butter round a shallow heat-proof dish. Place the scallops in the dish, pour over the wine and season well. Sprinkle over the breadcrumbs. Dot with the rest of the butter.
2. Cook in a moderate oven for 30 minutes. Serve straight from the dish.

Not suitable for freezing.

Can be prepared a few hours in advance until 2.

Hot

Seafood Kebabs

12 large scallops	1 lemon
½ kg. (1 lb. 2 oz.) peeled scampi	85 g. (3 oz.) butter
8 tomatoes	4 bayleaves
1 onion	seasoning
170 g. (6 oz.) small flat mushrooms	

Preparation

Wash the scallops, remove them from their shells and slice in half. Wash the tomatoes and cut in half. Peel the onion, then quarter, separating the layers. Wash the mushrooms and remove the stalks. Slice the lemon and cut the bayleaves in four.

Action

1. Put half a tomato on each skewer and then follow with alternate pieces of fish, onion, bayleaf, mushroom and lemon. End with half a tomato.
2. Melt the butter.

91

3. Place skewers under a hot grill for 8 minutes, pouring over the butter. Turn frequently and baste occasionally.

Not suitable for freezing.

Can be prepared a few hours in advance until 2.

Hot

The Great Chicken Dish

1 large chicken	60 g. (2 oz.) butter
¼ kg. (9 oz.) chicken livers	2 tablespoons oil
335 g. (¾ lb.) peeled prawns	1½ dl. (¼ pint) tomato juice
¼ kg. (9 oz.) cream cheese	¼ teaspoon Worcester sauce
8 fresh dates	seasoning
2 medium-sized November	
King cabbages	

Preparation

Remove any skin or fat from the chicken livers. Discard the outer purple leaves of the cabbages, then carefully cut off 24 leaves which should graduate from tea plate size to breakfast saucer size. Reserve the hearts of the cabbages for future use. Cut the dates in half, removing the stones and peeling off the skin.

Action

1. Rub a quarter of the butter into the chicken, season and roast in a moderate oven for 30 minutes so that it is partially cooked only. Cool slightly, remove skin and discard, then pull the chicken off the bone.

2. Put the chicken through a mincer with the chicken livers and the dates. Season.

3. Cook the cabbage leaves in boiling salted water for 2 minutes, then run under cold water.

4. Mix the prawns with the cream cheese, tomato juice and Worcester sauce.

5. Fill 16 of the leaves with the chicken mixture and 8 with the prawn and cream cheese mixture. Do this by rolling up the cabbage leaves, tucking in the ends and placing them face down on their join in a baking tin. Make certain that the chicken and prawn rolls are separate so that you will be able to serve each person with 2 chicken and 1 prawn.

6. Pour the oil over the cabbage rolls and dot with the remains of the butter and place in a slow oven for 40 minutes. The cream cheese will melt and should be poured over the rolls at the point of service.

Not suitable for freezing.

Can be prepared in advance until 6.

Hot

Warren Tandoori Chicken

2 small–medium chickens	2 teaspoons chilli powder
2 lemons	3 teaspoons ground coriander
6 tablespoons (approx.) oil	2 teaspoons ground cumin
3 dl. (½ pint) natural yoghourt	1 teaspoon ground ginger
4 tablespoons vinegar	1 teaspoon garam masala
a few drops orange food colouring	seasoning

Preparation

Skin the chickens and cut into large bite-size pieces. Squeeze the juice from the lemons.

Action

1. Mix together in a large bowl the yoghourt, vinegar, food colouring, spices and seasoning.

2. Place the chicken in the bowl. Cover and leave overnight if possible, but at least for 5 hours. Make sure all the pieces of chicken are well coated with the sauce.

3. Heat the oil in a frying-pan and sauté the chicken for 10 minutes turning the pieces frequently.

4. Transfer the contents of the frying-pan to a roasting tin and cook in a very moderate oven for 20 minutes. (The sauce will probably all have been absorbed, but coat the meat with any that is left before roasting.)

5. Sprinkle with the lemon juice and freshly ground black pepper before serving.

Not suitable for freezing.

Can be prepared in advance until 3.

Note: This makes a dry curry, so it is a good idea to serve it with a juicy salad. The one we suggest goes best with this dish is ¾ kg (1 lb. 11 oz.) tomatoes, mixed with about 2 tablespoons fresh chopped coriander leaves and stalks, 3 raw chillis finely chopped and seasoning. It should also be served with chapattis, chutney, boiled rice and any other side dishes you enjoy with curry.

Hot

New Year Chicken

8 half chicken breasts	2 dl. (⅓ pint) white wine
1 small cucumber	3 dl. (½ pint) double cream
3 Chinese gooseberries	½ teaspoon ground ginger
85 g. (3 oz.) butter	seasoning

Preparation

Remove the chicken from the bone and discard the skin, then cut into bite-size pieces. Peel and chop the cucumber. Skin and chop the Chinese gooseberries.

Action

1. Cook the chicken, cucumber, gooseberries and ginger with the butter over a low heat in a covered pan for 5 minutes. Shake occasionally.

2. Add the wine and seasoning and cook over a higher heat for a further 10 minutes. Remove from stove.

94

3. Stir in the cream and heat, but do not boil. Adjust seasoning and serve.

Not suitable for freezing.

Can be prepared in advance until 3.

Hot

Chicken West One

8 half chicken breasts	1 dl. (⅙ pint) sherry
450 g. (1 lb.) chicken livers	3 dl. (½ pint) double cream
335 g. (¾ lb.) mushrooms	seasoning
85 g. (3 oz.) butter	

Preparation

Remove the chicken from the bone and discard the skin. Cut into bite-size pieces. Wash and slice the mushrooms.

Action

1. Sauté the chicken and the chicken livers for 10 minutes in the butter, turning the meat occasionally so that it doesn't brown.

2. Add the mushrooms and seasoning and cook for a further 10 minutes.

3. Add the sherry and the cream. Heat but do not boil. Adjust seasoning and serve.

Suitable for freezing.

Can be prepared in advance.

Hot

Maltaise Chicken

10 half chicken breasts	*For the Hollandaise Sauce*
2 oranges	5 egg yolks
30 g. (1 oz.) butter	195 g. (7 oz.) butter
½ teaspoon lemon pepper	3 tablespoons water
seasoning	seasoning

G   95

Preparation

Remove the skin and bone from the chicken and cut into bite-size pieces. Grate the oranges, then squeeze them.

Action

1. Blanch the grated orange peel in boiling water for 2 minutes and strain through a piece of muslin.
2. Sauté the chicken in the butter with the lemon pepper for 8 minutes, turning the chicken over occasionally. The chicken should not be brown. Season. Transfer to a serving dish and keep warm.
3. Make the hollandaise sauce (p. 204). Add the orange juice and the grated peel, stir well, then add the chicken.

Not suitable for freezing.

Not suitable for advance preparation.

Hot

Tiller Chicken

10 chicken thighs	85 g. (3 oz.) butter
¼ kg. (9 oz.) back bacon	85 g. (3 oz.) flour
2 onions	¾ bottle red wine
¼ kg. (9 oz.) button mush-	2 dl. (⅓ pint) stock (p. 198)
rooms	4 bayleaves
6 cloves garlic	2 tcaspoons basil
2 sticks celery	seasoning
2 tablespoons oil	

Preparation

Peel and slice the onions. Peel and coarsely chop the garlic. Wash and slice the mushrooms. Trim, wash, scrape and slice the celery.

Action

1. Remove the rind and fry the bacon in its own fat for 10 minutes or until crisp. Remove from the pan and when cool break into small pieces.

2. Sauté the onions in the bacon fat for 10 minutes, adding a little of the oil if necessary.

3. Sauté the mushrooms in the rest of the oil for 7 minutes.

4. Place all the ingredients, except the butter and flour, in a casserole and cook in a moderate oven for 1 hour.

5. Strain the stock into a separate container and cool. It will take several hours for the fat to rise and solidify, when it should be scooped off and discarded.

6. Meanwhile keep the solid ingredients covered so that they will not dry. Remove the bayleaves and discard. Pull the flesh from the chicken, discarding the bones and skin.

7. Make a sauce with the butter, flour and stock (p. 203). When the sauce has boiled for 4 minutes, add all the other ingredients and cook for a further 5 minutes, or until really hot.

Suitable for freezing.

Can be prepared in advance.

Hot

Chicken Fricassee

1 capon or 2 small chickens	85 g. (3 oz.) flour
170 g. (6 oz.) baby carrots	2 tablespoons sherry
170 g. (6 oz.) button mush-rooms	4 egg yolks
2 tablespoons oil	3 dl. ($\frac{1}{2}$ pint) single cream
60 g. (2 oz.) butter	1$\frac{1}{2}$ litres (2 pints) water
	seasoning

Preparation

Top and tail the carrots and wash them. Wash the mushrooms.

Action

1. Cook the chickens with the bayleaves in the water for 1 hour, or 1$\frac{1}{2}$ hours if using a capon. Cool in the resulting stock. When the stock is cold remove the fat which will have formed on the surface.

2. Cook the carrots in water for 15 minutes.

3. Sauté the mushrooms for 5 minutes in the oil.

4. Remove the chicken from the bone, discarding the skin. Cut into bite-size pieces.

5. With the butter, flour and 8 dl. (1¼ pints) of the stock, make a sauce (p. 203). When the sauce has cooked for 4 minutes add the chicken, carrots, mushrooms and seasoning. Add the sherry. Remove from the heat and cool slightly, then add the egg yolks and stir in the cream. Heat but do not boil.

Not suitable for freezing.

Can be prepared in advance until the egg yolks and cream are added.

Hot

Martello Chicken

1 medium-sized cooked chicken	60 g. (2 oz.) butter
220 g. (½ lb.) brown and white crabmeat	2 dl. (⅓ pint) white wine
4 tomatoes	3 dl. (½ pint) double cream
220 g. (½ lb.) button mushrooms	2 tablespoons chopped parsley
	seasoning
	220 g. (½ lb.) flaky pastry (p. 196)

Preparation

Remove the chicken from the bone and cut into bite-size pieces, discarding the skin. Peel and chop the tomatoes. Wash the mushrooms. Cut the pastry into small squares, then place on a baking-tray.

Action

1. Simmer the crabmeat, tomatoes, parsley and wine in a covered pan for 5 minutes.

2. Put the contents of the pan into a blender or through a sieve. Season and return to the saucepan.

3. Sauté the mushrooms in the butter for 5 minutes, and then add to the crab sauce.

4. Cook the pastry in a hot oven for 10–15 minutes.

5. When the pastry is almost ready, add the chicken to the sauce and heat thoroughly. When the sauce is hot, remove from the heat and stir in the cream. Reheat but do not boil. Adjust the seasoning.

6. Put the mixture into a serving dish and decorate with the pastry cubes.

Suitable for freezing, but add the cream after defrosting, and cook the pastry freshly.

Can be prepared in advance, but cook pastry just before serving.

Hot

Spanish Main Chicken

6 chicken legs	2 dl. ($\frac{1}{3}$ pint) stock (p. 198)
220 g. ($\frac{1}{2}$ lb.) scallops	1 dessertspoon lemon juice
220 g. ($\frac{1}{2}$ lb.) calamari (squid)	$\frac{1}{2}$ teaspoon tarragon
450 g. (1 lb.) tomatoes	seasoning
450 g. (1 lb.) button onions	

Preparation

Clean the scallops. Remove the ink sacks, fins and skin from the calamari, turning them inside out to remove the bone and jelly from inside. Reserve the tentacles, which should be cut off just below the ink sacks, and put with the rest of the calamari. Peel and slice the tomatoes. Peel the onions.

Action

1. Place the chicken legs, stock, tomatoes, tarragon, seasoning and all but three of the onions in a casserole. Cover and cook in a moderate oven for 1 hour.

2. When the chicken is cool enough to handle, remove the skin and discard. Pull the flesh from the bones and return to the casserole to prevent it drying.

3. Simmer the fish, in sufficient water to cover, for 10 minutes with the remaining onions and the lemon juice. Drain and discard the onions. While the fish is still warm, cut the scallops into four and slice the calamari.

4. Put the contents of the casserole in a saucepan and add the fish. Bring to the boil, adjust seasoning and simmer for 3 minutes before serving.

Suitable for freezing.

Can be prepared in advance.

Hot

Chicken Jones

6 large chicken legs	60 g. (2 oz.) butter
670 g. (1½ lb.) leeks	seasoning

Preparation

Thoroughly wash and trim the leeks, discarding the dark green part, then slice the white part.

Action

1. Melt the butter in a large heavy saucepan. Add the leeks and shake, then pile the chicken legs on top. Cover the saucepan and place on a very low heat for 2 hours.

2. Pour the liquid into a bowl, and when cool place in the refrigerator. Leave the cover on the saucepan so that the chicken will not dry.

3. When the liquid has jellified, remove the layer of fat that will have formed, and discard.

4. Take the chicken from the pan. Discard the skin, then pull the chicken off the bone. Put the chicken pieces back in the saucepan, together with the jellied liquid. Adjust the seasoning and heat. Simmer for 4 minutes before serving.

Suitable for freezing.

Can be prepared in advance.

Cold

Chicken Mousse

1 large chicken
4 eggs
1 tablespoon oil
140 g. (5 oz.) butter
110 g. (¼ lb.) flour
3 dl. (½ pint) milk
1½ dl. (¼ pint) chicken stock
  (p. 199)

1 420 g. (15 oz.) tin
  consommé
1 dl. (⅙ pint) white wine
1½ dl. (¼ pint) double cream
1 tablespoon gelatin
1 sprig rosemary
seasoning

Preparation

Separate the eggs.

Action

1. Rub the oil into the skin of the chicken with some salt and pepper. Place 30 g. (1 oz.) of the butter and the rosemary inside the bird and roast in a moderate oven for 50–60 minutes.

2. Heat the consommé and dissolve the gelatin in it. Pour 2 dl. (⅓ pint) of it into a separate dish for use later as a glaze. Leave it all to cool.

3. Make a sauce with the butter, flour, milk, stock and unreserved consommé (p. 203). Boil for 5 minutes.

4. Remove the pan from the heat and mix a little of the sauce with the egg yolks, then tip the egg yolks into the sauce, together with the wine and seasoning. Make sure the sauce is not too hot or it will scramble the egg. Mix well and leave to cool.

5. When the chicken is cooked, take all the meat from the bones and discard the skin.

6. Place the chicken and sauce in a blender or Mouli and mix until smooth.

7. When the mixture from the blender is cool, stir in the cream. Stiffly beat the egg whites and fold in. Adjust the seasoning. Pour into a soufflé dish and leave to set in the refrigerator.

101

8. When the mousse has set, garnish with perhaps strips of cucumber peel and tomatoes to look like bunches of cherries or flowers. Spoon over the reserved consommé. It may be necessary to heat it again slightly, then to cool it to the right consistency, which is when it is *just* beginning to set. Chill in the refrigerator until required.

Suitable for freezing.

Can be prepared in advance.

Cold

Cherry and Bacon Chicken

8 half chicken breasts
220 g. (½ lb.) back bacon
220 g. (½ lb.) soft red cherries

1½ dl. (¼ pint) oil and
   vinegar dressing (p. 203)
1 bayleaf
seasoning

Preparation

Remove the stones from the cherries.

Action

1. Simmer the chicken breasts with the bayleaf, seasoning and sufficient water to cover for 35 minutes. Cool. Discard the bayleaf, strain the stock into a bowl for use in another recipe. Cut the chicken into bite-size pieces, removing any skin and bone.

2. Remove the rind, then grill the bacon until crisp. Cool and break into small pieces.

3. Mix the cherries with the bacon and the chicken. Season. Pour over the oil and vinegar dressing just before serving, and toss.

Not suitable for freezing.

Can be prepared in advance but do not dress until just before serving.

Cold

Celery and Pepper Chicken

8 half chicken breasts	1½ dl. (¼ pint) oil and vinegar
1 head celery	dressing (p. 203)
2 green peppers	½ teaspoon paprika
	seasoning

Preparation

Trim, wash and scrape the celery, then chop. Wash, deseed and slice the green pepper.

Action

1. Simmer the chicken breasts with seasoning, in enough water to cover, for 35 minutes. Cool, strain stock into a bowl for future use and cut chicken into bite-size pieces, removing the skin and any bone.
2. Mix the chicken with the celery and pepper, pour over the oil and vinegar dressing, toss and finally sprinkle with paprika.

Not suitable for freezing.

Can be prepared in advance but do not add dressing until the last moment.

Cold

Mushroom and Avocado Chicken

8 half chicken breasts	1½ dl. (¼ pint) oil and vinegar
220 g. (½ lb.) button	dressing (p. 203)
mushrooms	4 fresh basil leaves
2 avocado pears	1 bayleaf
¼ onion	seasoning

Preparation

Wash the mushrooms. Chop the basil. Peel and very finely chop the onion.

Action

1. Simmer the chicken breasts with the bayleaf, seasoning and

103

enough water to cover for 35 minutes. Cool, strain the stock into a bowl for future use, and discard the bayleaf. Cut the chicken into bite-size pieces, removing the skin and any bone

2. Cut the avocados in half, remove the stones, peel and slice Mix them and all the other ingredients carefully together with the chicken. Season and pour on the oil and vinegar dressing Turn over carefully before serving. Don't toss or the avocado will become mushy.

Not suitable for freezing.

Can be prepared in advance until 2.

Cold

Avocado and Grapefruit Chicken

8 half chicken breasts	4 dl. ($\frac{2}{3}$ pint) double cream
2 avocado pears	1 bayleaf
2 grapefruit	seasoning

Preparation

Peel the grapefruit, cutting deep through the pith to the fruit, then slice the fruit out of the segments. (It is easier to peel the grapefruit if you put them in water and bring them quickly to the boil then immediately afterwards put them in cold water.)

Action

1. Simmer the chicken breasts with the bayleaf, seasoning and enough water to cover for 35 minutes. Cool, discard the bayleaf, strain the stock into a bowl for future use and cut the chicken into bite-size pieces, removing the skin and any bone

2. Cut the avocado pears in half, remove the stones, peel and slice lengthways. Mix the chicken carefully with the avocado and the grapefruit. Season and pour over the cream. Do not toss or the avocado will go mushy.

Not suitable for freezing.

Can be prepared in advance but add the avocado and cream just before serving.

Cold

Floral Chicken

1 capon or large chicken	1 tablespoon chilli sauce
¼ kg. (9 oz.) peeled prawns	1 tablespoon Worcester sauce
3 globe artichokes	2 tablespoons lemon juice
3 dl. (½ pint) mayonnaise (p. 201)	⅛ teaspoon cayenne pepper seasoning

Preparation

Thoroughly wash the artichokes.

Action

1. Roast the capon or chicken in your favourite way (see next recipe), and cool completely.
2. Cook the artichokes in boiling salted water (to which you should add a few drops of oil to make the leaves separate), for approximately 45 minutes, or until the leaves pull out easily. Strain and cool slightly. When the artichokes are cool enough to handle comfortably, but not cold, carefully spread out the leaves so that it looks like an open flower, and remove the 'choke' completely. Put the flowers carefully on individual plates, covering them with wax paper to keep them moist if you will not be eating until later in the day.
3. Mix together the mayonnaise, chilli sauce, Worcester sauce, lemon juice and cayenne pepper. Do this very carefully, tasting all the time, otherwise you may get too hot a sauce for your taste; conversely some people may like to hot it up a bit.
4. Remove the capon or chicken from the bone, cut into bite-size pieces, discarding the skin, and mix with the prawns in the sauce. Adjust the seasoning.
5. Pile the chicken mixture into the centre of the artichokes.

Not suitable for freezing.

Can be prepared several hours in advance until 5.

Cold

Curried Chicken Mayonnaise

2 medium-sized chickens
1 small green pepper
1 small red pepper
4½ dl. (¾ pint) mayonnaise
  (p. 201)

1 level dessertspoon curry
  powder
seasoning

Preparation

Wash, deseed and finely chop the green and red peppers.

Action

1. Roast the chickens lightly in your favourite way. (Ours is the French method whereby you place the chicken with 60 g (2 oz.) butter and a tablespoon of oil and seasoning in a roasting tin in a cold oven. Switch on to maximum heat, and when this is reached turn down to very low and cook for a total of 1 hour from the moment the bird went into the oven for a medium-sized chicken. Larger ones take slightly longer.)
2. While the chicken is cooking, mix the curry powder with the mayonnaise, and stir in the peppers.
3. When the chicken is cooked, cool, remove from the bone and dice the meat, discarding the skin. Stir the meat into the mayonnaise, and adjust the seasoning and curry to taste.
4. Chill until required and serve attractively garnished.

Not suitable for freezing.

Can be prepared in advance.

Hot

Homeland Turkey

2 cold roast turkey legs from
  a medium-sized bird
3 large onions
3 green peppers
450 g. (1 lb.) mushrooms
3 tablespoons oil

60 g. (2 oz.) butter
1 tablespoon flour
3 dl. (½ pint) stock (p. 198)
2 dl. (⅓ pint) red wine
seasoning

Preparation

Cut the turkey meat off the bone, discarding the skin and the sinews in the drum stick. Cut into small pieces. Peel and chop the onions. Wash, deseed and slice the peppers. Wash the mushrooms and slice.

Action

. Sauté the onions in the oil in a covered pan for 5 minutes. Add the peppers and cook for a further 5 minutes. Add the mushrooms and cook for 5 minutes more, stirring occasionally.

. Make a white sauce with the butter, flour and stock (p. 203). When the sauce has boiled for 4 minutes add the wine and seasoning.

. Pour the sauce over the vegetables and simmer for 15 minutes, then add the turkey and continue to simmer for a further 15 minutes. Adjust the seasoning and serve.

Suitable for freezing.

Can be prepared in advance.

Cold

Lincolnshire Pheasant Salad

brace of pheasants	3 dl. (½ pint) commercially
head celery	soured cream
Cox's Orange Pippin apples	1 dessertspoon marmalade
0 g. (2 oz.) butter	1 dessertspoon curry powder
dl. (½ pint) water	1 bayleaf
dl. (½ pint) mayonnaise	seasoning
(p. 201)	

Preparation

Trim, wash, scrape and chop the celery.

Action

. Heat the butter in a heavy saucepan. Brown the pheasants, then turn them on to their breasts. Pour over the water, add

the bayleaf and seasoning. Cover and simmer gently for 4
minutes.

2. Remove the pheasants from the pan and leave to cool. Mean
while stir the curry powder into the juice. Boil uncovered unti
the quantity has reduced to about half. Extract the bayleaf an
stir in the marmalade until it has dissolved. Cool.

3. When the pheasant has cooled, take the meat from the bone
and dice, discarding the skin.*

4. When the juice is cool, mix it with the mayonnaise and sou
cream. Put the pheasant and celery in with it. Peel, core an
dice the apples and mix these in too. Stir well and adjust th
seasoning. Chill until required. Serve piled on to a plate an
attractively garnished to give it a little more colour.

Not suitable for freezing.

Can be prepared in advance.

*Note: A pheasant carcass makes excellent stock for soup, usin
the same method as for chicken stock, p. 199.

Hot

Rich and Rare Pheasant

3 hen pheasants	3 teaspoons lemon juice
450 g. (1 lb.) white grapes	$\frac{3}{4}$ bottle champagne
3 tablespoons oil	seasoning

Preparation

Peel and pip the grapes.

Action

1. Rub the pheasants with salt, the oil and the lemon juice an
either spit roast under a hot fire or grill for 20 minutes, so tha
the skin is brown and crisp but the flesh raw at the bone.

2. Cut the flesh from the bone into bite-size pieces, including th
fat and the crisp skin. Pull the flesh on the legs away from th
sinews. When the flesh has been removed from the body car

cass squeeze the carcass over the flesh, extracting as much of the blood as possible. Season.

3. Place the flesh in a large oven-proof dish and add the grapes and champagne. Place in a hot oven for 10 minutes, so that the pheasant is hot, but only cooks for about 2 minutes.

Not suitable for freezing.

Can be prepared in advance until 3.

Hot or cold

Pheasant Pie

brace pheasants	85 g. (3 oz.) butter
335 g. (¾ lb.) chicken livers	1 dl. (⅙ pint) sherry
10 g. (¼ lb.) sausage meat	4 egg yolks
2 onions	¼ teaspoon thyme
120 g. (¼ lb.) button mush-	2 bayleaves
rooms	seasoning
5 tablespoons oil	¼ kg. (9 oz.) shortcrust pastry
50 g. (2 oz.) flour	(p. 195)

Preparation

Remove any skin or fat from the chicken livers. Peel the onions, finely chop one and quarter the other. Wash and slice the mushrooms.

Action

1. Put the pheasants in a saucepan of water, two-thirds of the way up the sides of the birds. Add the quartered onion, thyme, bayleaves and seasoning. Simmer for 45 minutes. Meanwhile make the pastry if necessary, and put it to chill in the refrigerator.

2. While the pheasants are cooking, sauté the chicken livers and chopped onion in 3 tablespoons of the oil for 10 minutes. Put through a mincer and mix with the sausage meat.

3. Sauté the mushrooms in the other 2 tablespoons of oil.

4. When the pheasants are cooked, strain the stock into a jug.

109

Bone the birds, discarding the skin. Cut the flesh into small
pieces and place in a pie-dish.

5. Make a white sauce with the butter, flour and 6 dl. (1 pint) of
the stock (p. 203). When the sauce has boiled for 4 minutes
withdraw the pan from the heat and stir in the sherry. Mix a
little of the sauce with the egg yolks, then tip them into the
sauce, together with the mushrooms and the sausage meat
chicken liver mixture. Pour the sauce over the pheasant and
adjust seasoning.

6. Roll out the pastry to cover the dish, then bake in a moderately
hot oven for 35 minutes.

Suitable for freezing, preferably before cooking pastry.

Can be prepared in advance until 6.

Hot

Woodman's Prize

6 pigeons	1 bottle red wine
4 onions	3 teaspoons redcurrant jelly
1 head celery	4 bayleaves
335 g. (¾ lb.) mushrooms	seasoning
1½ dl. (¼ pint) oil	

Preparation

Remove the meat from the pigeons, cutting into bite-size pieces
Peel and slice the onions. Trim, wash, scrape and slice the celery
Wash and slice the mushrooms.

Action

1. Marinate everything except the mushrooms in the wine and all
but 2 tablespoons of the oil for 6 hours.

2. Sauté the mushrooms in the reserved oil for 10 minutes.

3. Mix the mushrooms with the other ingredients and place in a
casserole in a moderate oven for 1¼ hours.

Suitable for freezing, but remove the bayleaves first.

Can be prepared in advance.

Hot

Rabbit and Prune Stew

1¼ kg. (2¾ lb.) cut rabbit	2 cloves garlic
or 2 wild rabbits	1½ dl. (¼ pint) oil
195 g. (7 oz.) back bacon	1 bottle red wine
20 vacuum-packed stoned	2 tablespoons chopped parsley
prunes	¼ teaspoon thyme
2 onions	1 bayleaf
2 carrots	seasoning

Preparation

Remove rind and chop the bacon. Cut the prunes in half. Peel and chop the onions. Scrape and slice the carrots. Peel and slice the garlic.

Action

1. Put everything except the prunes in a bowl and marinate for 6 hours or more.
2. Remove the bayleaf, then put everything else that has been marinated into a casserole and cook in a moderate oven for 1 hour. Cool.
3. Take the rabbit from the casserole and pull the flesh from the bones, discarding the sinews.
4. Place the other cooked ingredients in a blender, or mince and sieve them.
5. Before serving, put the rabbit and the blended bacon and vegetables into a saucepan and bring to the boil. Add the prunes, which should be heated but not cooked. Adjust seasoning.

Suitable for freezing, but add the prunes after defrosting.

Can be prepared in advance until 5.

Note: Ordinary dried prunes, even if soaked, are not ideal for this dish.

Cold

Mustard Veal

¾ kg. (1 lb. 11 oz.) fillet of veal
¾ kg. (1 lb. 11 oz.) tomatoes
220 g. (½ lb.) button mush-
　rooms
8 fresh basil leaves
60 g. (2 oz.) butter
1 dl. (⅙ pint) white wine
2 tablespoons French mustard
2 dessertspoons tomato purée
3 dl. (½ pint) aspic
1 teaspoon lemon pepper
seasoning

For the Brown Sauce
1 large onion
1 carrot
4 rashers streaky bacon
reserved mushroom stalks
60 g. (2 oz.) butter
85 g. (3 oz.) flour
9 dl. (1½ pints) stock (p. 198)
seasoning

Preparation

Slice the veal and bang flat. Peel the tomatoes and chop in half if
small, or in quarters if large. Wash the mushrooms and reserve
the stalks for the sauce. Peel and chop the onion. Scrape and chop
the carrot. Dice the bacon. Make up the aspic, following the
directions on the packet, and leave to cool.

Action

1. Make the brown sauce (p. 204), adding the bacon and mushroom stalks at the beginning with the onion and carrot. Strain.
   Add the wine, then return to the pan, and reduce the quantity
   by one-third, by cooking over a moderate heat. When this has
   been done, stir in the mustard, tomato purée and lemon pepper.
   Season and cool.

2. Dot the veal with 30 g. (1 oz.) of the butter and the basil and
   put under a hot grill for 1 minute on each side. Cool, discard
   the basil leaves, and cut the meat into bite-size pieces, removing
   any fat.

3. Sauté the mushrooms very lightly in the remains of the butter.
   Cool.

4. Arrange the veal, tomatoes and mushrooms in a shallow dish. Pour over the sauce, making the surface as smooth as possible. Allow to cool completely, and then spoon over the aspic when it is just beginning to set (p. 199).

Not suitable for freezing.

Can be prepared in advance.

Hot

Kirsch Veal

900 g. (2 lb.) fillet of veal
450 g. (1 lb.) lambs' sweetbreads
1 small pineapple
30 g. (1 oz.) butter

4 tablespoons Kirsch
3 dl. ($\frac{1}{2}$ pint) double cream
1$\frac{1}{2}$ dl. ($\frac{1}{4}$ pint) stock (p. 198)
seasoning

Preparation

Slice and bang the veal flat. Trim the fat from the sweetbreads. Peel the pineapple and remove the core. Slice into small pieces.

Action

1. Heat the butter in a frying-pan and sauté the sweetbreads in it for 15 minutes.

2. Meanwhile put the veal under a hot grill for 1 minute on each side. Trim off the fat and cut into bite-size pieces.

3. Add the veal to the sweetbreads. Pour in the stock, and when hot add the pineapple and seasoning. Heat the pineapple, but don't cook it.

4. Add the Kirsch and cream at the point of service, and heat but do not boil. Adjust seasoning.

Not suitable for freezing.

Not suitable for advance preparation.

Hot

Courgette Veal Hollandaise

670 g. (1½ lb.) fillet of veal
½ kg. (1 lb. 2 oz.) firm young
  courgettes
60 g. (2 oz.) butter
3 dl. (½ pint) mild stock (p.
  198)
seasoning

For the Hollandaise Sauce
5 egg yolks
195 g. (7 oz.) butter
3 tablespoons water
seasoning

Preparation

Trim the veal and cut into small pieces. Bang flat. Wash and top and tail the courgettes and cut each into about 5 pieces.

Action

1. Simmer the courgettes in the stock in a covered pan for about 8 minutes. Drain and leave covered.
2. Lightly fry the veal in the butter and place with the courgettes in a serving dish to keep warm in the oven. Season lightly.
3. Make the hollandaise sauce (p. 204). Pour it over the veal and courgettes. Serve immediately.

Not suitable for freezing.

Not suitable for advance preparation.

Hot

Keller Veal

900 g. (2 lb.) pie veal
450 g. (1 lb.) Frankfurter
  sausages
220 g. (½ lb.) kohlrabi

2 continental radishes
6 dl. (1 pint) bitter beer
1 dessertspoon French mustard
seasoning

Preparation

Chop the veal. Slice the Frankfurters. Wash the kohlrabi. Wash the radishes and top and tail them, then chop each into about ten pieces.

Action

1. Boil the kohlrabi for 20 minutes in salted water, then slice. The purpose of this is that kohlrabi can be woody, particularly towards the centre, and any pieces which do not have the texture of a peach should be discarded.

2. Put the veal, sausage, kohlrabi, radish and mustard, mixed with the beer, into a casserole. Season and place in a moderate oven for 1½ hours. Should the veal be of poor quality with fat and gristle, then cook the dish for up to 3 hours, but check the liquid after the first 2 hours and add more beer if necessary.

Suitable for freezing.

Can be prepared in advance.

Hot

Citrus Rissoles

900 g. (2 lb.) good quality pie veal	2 dl. (⅓ pint) milk
2 eggs	½ teaspoon Worcester sauce
1 orange	¼ teaspoon ground nutmeg
2 slices white bread	small pinch thyme
4 tablespoons oil	½ teaspoon paprika
60 g. (2 oz.) butter	seasoned flour (p. 198)
	seasoning

Preparation

Remove all fat and skin from the meat. Beat the eggs. Peel the orange, removing all the pith, and cut the flesh from the inner skins. Cut the crusts from the bread.

Action

1. Mince the veal finely with the bread.

2. Put the minced mixture into a large bowl and add the eggs, milk, Worcester sauce, nutmeg, thyme, paprika and seasoning.

3. Press the mixture into rissoles, placing half an orange segment in the centre of each.

115

4. Roll carefully in the seasoned flour and fry for 7 minutes on each side in the butter and oil.

Suitable for freezing, preferably before cooking.

Can be prepared in advance until 4.

Cold

Lamb Terrine

1 kg. (2¼ lb.) piece of leg of lamb
½ kg. (1 lb. 2 oz.) chicken livers
1 onion
2 tablespoons oil
1 dl. (⅛ pint) red wine

3 dl. (½ pint) aspic
1 tablespoon rosemary jelly or 1 tablespoon redcurrant jelly and a sprig of rosemary
1 bayleaf
seasoning

Preparation

Remove all the fat from the lamb and discard, then cut the meat from the bone and slice into pieces the size of large sugar lumps. Peel and chop the onion. Remove any skin or fat from the chicken livers. Make up the aspic, following the directions on the packet.

Action

1. Sauté the chicken livers with the chopped onion in the oil for 10 minutes. Cool and put them through a mincer.
2. Place the bayleaf and the rosemary, if not using rosemary jelly, on the bottom of a fireproof terrine. Mix the lamb with the chicken livers, onion and seasoning and press into the dish. If using rosemary jelly, spoon over the top, or redcurrant jelly if using that. Pour on the wine.
3. Cover the dish and place in a moderate oven for 20 minutes, then remove the cover and continue to cook in a slow oven for 2 hours. Cool and turn out. Remove the rosemary and bayleaf. Garnish attractively and spoon over the aspic (p. 199).

Suitable for freezing, but it is better to decorate and glaze after defrosting.

Can be prepared in advance.

Hot

Lamb Soubise

1 kg. (2¼ lb.) lamb fillet

For the Marinade
4 tablespoons oil
4 tablespoons red wine
4 juniper berries
lemon pepper
½ teaspoon salt
4 cloves

For the Soubise Sauce
2 onions
85 g. (3 oz.) butter
60 g. (2 oz.) flour
6 dl. (1 pint) milk
2 tablespoons single cream
seasoning

2 tablespoons oil for frying

Preparation

Cut the lamb into bite-size pieces. Crush the juniper berries and mix together all the marinade ingredients. Leave the meat to marinate for at least 6 hours, turning from time to time. Peel and finely chop the onions.

Action

1. Blanch the onions in boiling water for 5 minutes, then drain.
2. Heat one-third of the butter in a small saucepan and sauté the onions until soft, but not brown. Sieve or blend the onions to make a purée.
3. Make a white sauce with the butter, flour and milk (p. 203). When the sauce has boiled for 4 minutes, stir in the onion purée and season well. Leave simmering very gently.
4. Strain the marinade into a jug and discard the juniper berries and cloves.
5. Heat the oil in a large frying-pan and cook the meat over a high heat for 5 minutes, stirring frequently to seal.
6. Pour over the marinade, reduce the heat slightly, and cook for a further 7 minutes, or longer if you like your lamb well done.
7. Lift the meat out of the pan with a draining spoon, and put into a heated serving dish.

8. Stir the cream into the sauce. Warm but do not boil. Adjust the seasoning, and pour over the meat.

Marinated meat and sauce suitable for freezing separately.

Can be prepared in advance until 5 but don't leave the sauce simmering.

Hot

Burlington Lamb

1 kg. (2¼ lb.) lamb from the top of the leg	1½ dl. (¼ pint) oil
16 lambs' kidneys	¾ bottle red wine
2 cloves garlic	½ teaspoon paprika
85 g. (3 oz.) butter	1 teaspoon basil
	seasoning

Preparation

Cut the lamb into bite-size pieces, discarding any fat and skin. Skin the kidneys and core, then slice into four or five rounds. Peel and chop the garlic.

Action

1. Marinate the lamb overnight in the oil and wine, together with the garlic, basil, paprika and seasoning.

2. Sauté the kidneys in the butter for 6 minutes, turning. Remove from pan.

3. Take the lamb out of the marinade and fry without oil in a very hot pan for 3 minutes, turning frequently to prevent the meat sticking.

4. Add the kidneys to the lamb, together with the marinade, and cook for a further 3 minutes. Adjust seasoning.

Not suitable for freezing.

Not suitable for advance preparation beyond marination.

Hot

Lamb Kebabs

2 kg. (4½ lb.) leg of lamb
8 tomatoes
3 green peppers
170 g. (6 oz.) small flat
  mushrooms
2 bayleaves

For the Marinade
3 dl. (½ pint) red wine
6 tablespoons oil
1 clove garlic
1 bayleaf
¼ teaspoon each of thyme,
  rosemary and tarragon
seasoning

Preparation

Bone the leg of lamb, removing all the fat and sinews. Cut the meat into bite-size pieces. Wash the tomatoes and cut in half. Wash and deseed the peppers, then cut them into bite-size pieces. Wash the mushrooms and remove the stalks. Cut the 2 bayleaves into four. Peel and crush the garlic.

Action

1. Mix together all the marinade ingredients and place the lamb in it for 2 hours.
2. Put half a tomato on each skewer and then follow with alternate pieces of meat, pepper and mushrooms, with a piece of bayleaf placed towards the middle. End with half a tomato.
3. Place the skewers under a hot grill for 10 minutes, turning frequently. Baste generously during cooking with the marinade.

Not suitable for freezing.

Can be prepared a few hours in advance until 3.

Hot

Nippon Lamb

12 lamb chump chops
4 onions
¾ kg. (1¾ lb.) green cabbage
4 tablespoons oil

1 teaspoon lemon juice
½ teaspoon chilli powder
seasoning

119

Preparation

Cut the bone from the chops. Peel the onions and slice them finely. Discard the outer leaves of the cabbage, and wash and slice the remainder.

Action

1. Rub the lemon juice on the chops, season and place under a hot grill so that the fat is uppermost. Cook for 5 minutes until the fat has become brown and crisp. Now cut the chops into bite-size pieces.
2. Using two frying-pans, fry the onions in the oil for 2 minutes, so that they are still white but just beginning to soften. Add the cabbage and mix well. Season. Cook together for 3 minutes.
3. Meanwhile grill the pieces of lamb for 4 minutes, turning in the grill tray so that the fire reaches all sides of the meat, which should remain pink inside.
4. Add the chilli powder to the vegetables and mix in the meat. Serve immediately and do not overcook as the cabbage and onions must still be crisp.

Not suitable for freezing.

Not suitable for advance preparation.

Hot

Right Bank Lamb

¾ kg. (1 lb. 11 oz.) fillet of lamb	8 potatoes
2 large onions	¼ kg. (9 oz.) French beans
2 cloves garlic	60 g. (2 oz.) butter
¼ kg. (9 oz.) tomatoes	4 dl. (⅔ pint) stock (p. 198)
1 head celery	½ teaspoon thyme
	seasoning

Preparation

Cut the meat into cubes. Peel and slice the onions and tomatoes. Peel and crush the garlic. Trim, wash, scrape and slice the celery. Peel and quarter the potatoes. String and cut the beans, if not using frozen ones.

Action

1. Heat the butter in a heavy saucepan and fry the onions until brown, but not burnt.
2. Add the lamb, garlic and thyme, and brown.
3. Add the tomatoes, celery, stock and plenty of seasoning. Cover and cook over a very low heat for 1 hour. Stir frequently.
4. Add the potatoes. Cover and cook for a further 20 minutes.
5. Add the French beans, adjust the seasoning. Cover and cook for a further 15 minutes.

Suitable for freezing, preferably before stage 4.

Can be prepared in advance until 5.

Hot

Hot Pot

1 kg. (2¼ lb.) leg of lamb	4 prunes
6 lambs' kidneys	3 tablespoons oil
4 onions	30 g. (1 oz.) butter
¾ kg. (1¾ lb.) potatoes	30 g. (1 oz.) flour
¼ kg. (9 oz.) mushrooms	2 dl. (⅓ pint) red wine
220 g. (½ lb.) tin of globe artichoke hearts	2 dl. (⅓ pint) stock (p. 198)
	seasoning

Preparation

Cut the meat from the bone, discarding any skin and fat, and slice. Skin, core and chop the kidneys. Peel the onions, slice three of them and finely chop the fourth. Peel and slice the potatoes the thickness of a 50p. piece. Wash the mushrooms. Cut the artichoke hearts in half. Soak the prunes for 2 hours unless using vacuum-packed ones.

Action

1. Sauté the kidney with the finely chopped onion in 1 tablespoon of the oil for 5 minutes.
2. With the butter, flour and stock make a white sauce (p. 203).

121

When the sauce has cooked for 4 minutes add the onion and kidney.

3. Place a layer of potatoes in a large oven-proof dish. On this place alternate layers of lamb and kidney mixture, scattering both with the mushrooms, sliced onions, artichokes and more of the potato, leaving enough to layer the top. Season each layer.

4. Add the chopped prunes and pour over the wine. Place a layer of potatoes carefully over the top, season them and cover with the remaining oil.

5. Cook in a moderate oven for 2 hours.

Not suitable for freezing.

Can be prepared in advance.

Hot

Hop Garden Lamb

2 kg. (4½ lb.) cheap cuts of lamb
4 large onions

6 dl. (1 pint) bitter beer or pale ale
1 teaspoon paprika seasoning

Preparation

Cut all the skin and fat from the lamb and discard. Cut the lean meat from any bone, and slice into bite-size pieces. (There is so little lean meat on cheap cuts of lamb that you are unlikely to find you have large enough pieces to slice.) You should be left with about 900 g. (2 lb.) of lean lamb. Peel and slice the onions.

Action

Put the lamb in a casserole with the onions, and pour over the beer. Season and dust with the paprika. Cover and cook in a slow oven for 2 hours.

Suitable for freezing.

Can be prepared in advance.

Note: This is a very good way of using up all those bits of a half sheep you don't know what to do with, and which take up valuable space in the freezer. If you haven't bought half a sheep, then ask your butcher for 5 small breasts of lamb, or what he judges to be the equivalent in the cheapest cuts.

Hot

Shepherds in Arcadia Pie

670 g. (1½ lb.) boned cold roast lamb	8 fresh dates
335 g. (¾ lb.) chicken livers	4 tablespoons oil
½ kg. (1 lb. 2 oz.) onions	2 dessertspoons honey
5 potatoes	1½ dl. (¼ pint) single cream
335 g. (¾ lb.) tomatoes	seasoning

Preparation

Remove any skin or fat from the lamb and chicken livers. Peel and chop the onions. Peel the potatoes. Skin and chop the tomatoes. Cut open the dates, remove the stones, skin and chop them. Mix the honey with the cream.

Action

1. Using half the oil, sauté the chicken livers and about a quarter of the onions for 10 minutes, then put through a mincer, together with the lamb.

2. Sauté the rest of the onions in the remaining oil until they begin to brown, about 10 minutes. Boil the potatoes in salted water in the ordinary way and drain and mash when cooked.

3. Add the other ingredients, except the potatoes, to the onions, and season. Cook over a low heat for 20 minutes.

4. Place the meat mixture in a fire-proof dish and top with the mashed potato. Place in a moderate oven for 35 minutes.

Suitable for freezing.

Can be prepared in advance.

123

Hot

Beef Stroganoff

1 kg. (2¼ lb.) good rump
 or fillet steak
3 onions
335 g. (¾ lb.) button mushrooms
170 g. (6 oz.) butter

3 dl. (½ pint) commercially
 soured cream
¼ teaspoon freshly grated
 nutmeg
seasoning

Preparation

Trim any fat and gristle from the steak, then cut it across the grain
into slices 1·25 cm. (½ in.) wide and about 3·75 cm. (1½ in.) long
then bang these out flat. Peel and finely chop the onions. Wash and
slice the mushrooms.

Action

1. Heat half the butter in a large heavy frying-pan and cook the
   onions for about 15 minutes until they are soft and very slightly
   browned. Add the mushrooms and cook for a further 5 minutes
   stirring regularly. Sprinkle over a little salt and plenty of
   freshly ground black pepper. Remove from pan.
2. Heat the rest of the butter in the frying-pan and cook the meat
   for 4 minutes, stirring so that it all gets cooked.
3. Return the mushrooms and onions to the pan. Cover and cook
   very gently for 15 minutes, stirring occasionally.
4. Stir in the sour cream and heat thoroughly, but without allowing
   the cream to boil. Sprinkle with grated nutmeg.

Suitable for freezing, but better to add the sour cream after de
frosting.

Better prepared fresh but can be prepared in advance until 4.

Note: This dish is best served with plain boiled rice.

Hot

Summit Steak

1 kg. (2¾ lb.) best fillet steak	¾ dl. (⅛ pint) dry vermouth
3 dessertspoons crumbled	1 dessertspoon lemon juice
Danish blue cheese	1 tablespoon chopped parsley
3 dl. (1 pint) commercially	seasoning
soured cream	

Preparation

Remove all fat from the meat and cut into bite-size pieces. Sprinkle on the lemon juice and seasoning.

Action

1. Put the steak in a hot frying-pan and cook for about 2 minutes, turning the pieces to prevent them from sticking.
2. In a separate pan heat the cream and the vermouth and when hot, but not boiling, add the cheese and parsley. Season.
3. Put the steak in a serving dish and pour over the sauce.

Not suitable for freezing.

Not suitable for advance preparation.

Hot

Tennessee Beef Wonder

900 g. (2 lb.) good braising	3 dl. (½ pint) stock (p. 198)
steak	2 dl. (⅓ pint) white wine
220 g. (½ lb.) lean ham	1 dl. (⅙ pint) oil and vinegar
lettuce	dressing (p. 203)
450 g. (1 lb.) onions	1 bayleaf
220 g. (½ lb.) mushrooms	seasoning
140 g. (5 oz.) tomatoes	

Preparation

Cut the fat from the beef and bang flat. Slice the beef and the ham into strips. Wash the lettuce. Peel and chop the onions. Wash and slice the mushrooms. Peel and slice the tomatoes.

Action

1. Toss the lettuce in the oil and vinegar dressing and leave to marinate for 1 hour. (Obviously this is a good way to use up a salad. Cut the leaves into two or three pieces.

2. Put all the ingredients into a casserole, season and cook in a moderate oven for 1½ hours.

Suitable for freezing.

Can be prepared in advance.

Hot

Chilli Beef

1 kg. (2¼ lb.) best quality fresh minced beef	4 tablespoons Bourbon whisky (optional)
5 onions	2 teaspoons chilli powder
4 cloves garlic	½ teaspoon thyme
1 large tin kidney beans	½ teaspoon basil
1 large red pepper	¼ teaspoon cayenne pepper
3 tablespoons oil	¼ teaspoon paprika
5 tablespoons tomato purée	4 bayleaves
3 dl. (½ pint) stock (p. 198)	seasoning

Preparation

Skin and roughly chop the onions. Skin and finely chop the garlic. Wash, deseed and chop the pepper (green will do if red are not available). Mix the chilli powder with the stock.

Action

1. Heat the oil in a large heavy saucepan and sauté the onions and garlic for 5 minutes. Add the meat and brown it.

2. Add all the other ingredients to the meat and onions. Season and stir well. Cover the pan and simmer over a very low heat for 1¼ hours, stirring occasionally. Adjust seasoning before serving.

Suitable for freezing.

Can be prepared in advance.

126

Hot

Root Beef

¾ kg. (1 lb. 11 oz.) sliced
    topside of beef
6 sticks celery
2 leeks
2 large onions
¼ kg. (9 oz.) young carrots
30 g. (1 oz.) mixed dried fruit

2 tablespoons oil
1½ dl. (¼ pint) tomato ketchup
1½ dl. (¼ pint) water
4 tablespoons wine vinegar
2 tablespoons Worcester sauce
2 tablespoons brown sugar
seasoning

Preparation

Trim the meat and cut into bite-size pieces. Trim, wash, scrape and slice the celery. Thoroughly wash and trim the leeks, removing the dark green part, then slice the white parts. Skin and chop the onions. Scrape the carrots and cut into rounds.

Action

1. Heat the oil in a frying-pan and sauté the beef for 5 minutes. Add the celery, leeks and onions and cook for a further 5 minutes.
2. Stir in all the other ingredients and season well. Cover the pan and simmer for 30 minutes.
3. Transfer the contents of the pan to a casserole and cook in a moderate oven for 45 minutes.

Suitable for freezing.

Can be prepared in advance.

Hot or cold

Seville Beef

¾ kg. (1 lb. 11 oz.) cold roast
    beef
335 g. (¾ lb.) tomatoes
1 green pepper
450 g. (1 lb.) pre-cooked globe
    artichoke hearts
12 black olives

4 tablespoons chopped celery
3 dl. (½ pint) stock (p. 198)
3 dl. (½ pint) single cream
1 tablespoon marmalade
1 tablespoon curry powder
seasoning

I   127

Preparation

Remove any fat from the beef and cut the meat into small cubes
Peel and chop the tomatoes. Wash, deseed and slice the pepper
Stone the olives and chop.

Action

1. Simmer the tomatoes in the stock for 5 minutes. Stir in the
   curry powder. Season and withdraw the pan from the heat.
2. Add the meat, pepper, artichoke hearts, black olives and
   marmalade. Leave overnight, or for several hours, having
   cooled and placed in a covered bowl in the refrigerator. (This
   allows the flavours to develop.)
3. Return to the saucepan and heat, stirring regularly. At the
   point of service, add the chopped celery, and stir in the cream
   Adjust the seasoning. Serve hot, or cool, chill and serve cold

Not suitable for freezing.

Can be prepared in advance.

Hot

Cider Vinegar Stew

900 g. (2 lb.) round eye of
    steak
3 large onions
220 g. (½ lb.) mushrooms
4 tablespoons oil

3 dl. (½ pint) mild stock (p.
    198)
4 tablespoons cider vinegar
4 dl. (⅔ pint) single cream
seasoned flour (p. 198)
seasoning

Preparation

Trim any fat off the steak and cut into narrow strips. Coat the
meat with the seasoned flour. Peel and chop the onions. Wash the
mushrooms.

Action

1. Put the onion with the oil in a covered pan and sauté for 10
   minutes.

128

2. Add the beef and cook for a further 5 minutes, shaking the pan occasionally.

3. Add the stock and vinegar and cook for a further 20 minutes.

4. Add the mushrooms, adjust the seasoning and continue cooking for 10 minutes. At the point of service, stir in the cream, heat, but do not boil.

Suitable for freezing before adding the cream.

Can be prepared in advance but add cream at the end.

Hot

Mock Sukiyaki

900 g. (2 lb.) sliced topside of beef	4 tablespoons oil
1 small head celery	¾ litre (1¼ pints) good home-made consommé (p. 55) or
¼ kg. (9 oz.) button mush-rooms	2 tins condensed consommé
1 large green pepper	2 tablespoons soy sauce
2 large onions	4 tablespoons cornflour
12 spring onions	seasoning
6 water chestnuts	rice

Preparation

Trim the meat and cut into thin strips. Trim, wash, scrape and slice the celery. Wash and slice the mushrooms. Wash, deseed and chop the green pepper. Peel and slice the onions and spring onions, including part of the green tops of the latter. Slice the water chestnuts. Mix the cornflour to a smooth paste with about 1½ dl. (¼ pint) of cold water.

Action

1. Heat the oil in a large frying-pan (use two if necessary), and brown the meat. At the same time put on some salted water to boil for the rice and cook for 15 minutes, drain and put into a heated dish. It is quite nice to have the brown rice which is now available, but this takes 50 minutes to cook, but adequate

time should be allowed, so you don't have to keep the meat waiting.

2. Add all the vegetables, water chestnuts, consommé, soy sauce and seasoning to the meat. Cover and cook over a low heat for 12 minutes, stirring frequently until the vegetables are *just* tender.

3. Add the cornflour mixture and stir until the sauce has thickened and cook for 4 minutes.

4. Serve surrounded by the rice, or separately, as you prefer.

Not suitable for freezing.

Not suitable for advance preparation.

Hot

Rissoles

¾ kg. (1 lb. 11 oz.) cooked minced beef*
2 onions
60 g. (2 oz.) butter
60 g. (2 oz.) flour
2 dl. (⅓ pint) strong stock (p. 199)
1 dessertspoon tomato purée

1 dessertspoon Worcester sauce
½ teaspoon mixed herbs seasoning
2 eggs and browned breadcrumbs for coating
oil for frying

Preparation

Peel and finely chop the onions.

Action

1. Heat the butter in a saucepan and cook the onions until well browned.

2. Sprinkle over the flour and cook for 2 minutes. Blend in the stock, tomato purée, Worcester sauce and herbs. Bring to the boil and cook for 4 minutes.

3. Withdraw the pan from the heat, stir in the meat and season well. Transfer to a bowl and leave to get quite cold.

4. When cold, divide into 16 equal portions and shape on a well floured board.
5. Coat in beaten egg and breadcrumbs and fry until well browned on each side.

Suitable for freezing, preferably before frying.

Can be prepared in advance until 5.

Note: See recipe for consommé on p. 55.

Hot

Hamburgers

¾ kg. (1 lb. 11 oz.) best
   quality fresh minced beef
8 baps
2 eggs
2 onions
2 tablespoons oil

1 tablespoon horseradish
   sauce
2 teaspoons Worcester sauce
1 teaspoon curry powder
½ teaspoon thyme
seasoning

Preparation

Slit the baps in half. Peel and very finely chop the onions.

Action

1. Mix together the beef, eggs, onions, horeseradish sauce, Worcester sauce, curry powder, thyme and seasoning. Divide into 8 equal portions and shape each one into a round ball, then press flat so that the hamburger is about 2 cm. (¾ in.) thick.
2. Heat the oil in a frying-pan and cook to suit your guests' tastes. As a rough guide, a hamburger cooked for 10 minutes on each side will be well done, 6 minutes medium, and 3 minutes rare.
3. Place the hamburgers in the split buns with perhaps lettuce, mayonnaise, tomato ketchup, mustard, pickles, or anything else you like.

Hamburger mixture (before cooking) and baps both suitable for freezing separately.

Can be prepared in advance until 2.

131

Hot

Steak, Kidney and Prune Casserole

900 g. (2 lb.) stewing steak
8 lambs' kidneys
10 prunes
110 g. (¼ lb.) back bacon
¼ kg. (9 oz.) flat mushrooms
6 onions
3 carrots

2 tomatoes
4 tablespoons oil
1 litre (1¾ pints) stock (p. 198)
3 bayleaves
seasoned flour (p. 198)
seasoning

Preparation

Trim and chop the stewing steak. Skin and core the kidneys, cutting each into six pieces. Coat the steak and kidneys with the seasoned flour. Soak the prunes for at least 1½ hours. Wash and chop the mushrooms. Peel and quarter the onions. Cut the rind from the bacon and chop the meat. Scrape the carrots and chop. Peel and slice the tomatoes.

Action

1. Fry the bacon lightly in its own fat and remove. Brown the steak, in the bacon fat, adding some of the oil. When the steak has browned, remove from the frying-pan.

2. Brown the kidneys in the remainder of the oil. Finally sauté the mushrooms.

3. Place all the meat and vegetables in a large saucepan with the bayleaves and seasoning. Cover with the stock and simmer for 2 hours with the lid on.

4. After 1½ hours, stone the prunes, cut them in half and add to the stew.

Suitable for freezing.

Can be prepared in advance.

Hot

No Pie Steak and Kidney

900 g. (2 lb.) good stewing
  steak
¼ kg. (9 oz.) ox kidney or
  lambs' kidneys
2 large onions
6 medium carrots

3 tablespoons oil
3 dl. (½ pint) stock
1 teaspoon mixed tarragon,
  thyme and basil
seasoned flour (p. 198)
seasoning

Preparation

Trim all the fat and gristle from the steak and cut into cubes. Cut
the kidney from the core, skin and cube. Peel and slice the onions
and carrots. Mix the seasoned flour with the herbs. Coat the steak
and kidney well with the mixture.

Action

1. Heat the oil in a heavy frying-pan and sauté the onions for 7
   minutes. Add the steak and kidney and cook for 10 minutes,
   stirring regularly so that all the meat is sealed.
2. Add the carrots and blend in the stock. Bring to the boil,
   adjust seasoning and transfer to a casserole dish.
3. Cook in a low oven for 2 hours.

Suitable for freezing.
Can be prepared in advance.

Hot

Beef and Kidney Kebabs

670 g. (1½ lb.) rump steak
8 large lambs' kidneys
8 tomatoes
3 green peppers
170 g. (6 oz.) small flat
  mushrooms
1 onion
2 bayleaves

For the Marinade
1½ dl. (¼ pint) red wine
3 tablespoons oil
1 clove garlic
1 bayleaf
¼ teaspoon each of thyme and
  tarragon
seasoning

Preparation

Remove any fat from the steak and cut into bite-size pieces. Core and skin the kidneys and cut each into four. Wash the tomatoes and cut in half. Wash and deseed the peppers then cut them into bite-size pieces. Wash the mushrooms and remove the stalks. Peel the onion, then quarter, separating the layers. Cut the bay-leaves in four. Peel and crush the garlic.

Action

1. Mix together all the marinade ingredients and place the beef in the marinade for 2 hours.
2. Put half a tomato on each skewer and then follow with alternate pieces of beef, pepper, kidney, mushroom and onion, with a piece of bayleaf near the middle. End with half a tomato.
3. Place the skewers under a hot grill for 10 minutes and pour over some of the marinade. Turn frequently and baste occasionally.

Not suitable for freezing.

Can be prepared a few hours in advance until 3.

Hot

Goulash

450 g. (1 lb.) stewing steak	1 handful macaroni
450 g. (1 lb.) fillet of pork	4 tablespoons oil
2 large onions	9 dl. (1½ pints) water
3 large red peppers	seasoned flour (p. 198)
450 g. (1 lb.) potatoes	seasoning

Preparation

Remove all fat from the meat and cut into bite-size pieces. Peel and chop the onions. Wash, deseed and chop the peppers. Peel and slice the potatoes. Toss the meat in the seasoned flour.

Action

1. Sauté the onions and peppers in the oil in a large covered saucepan for 10 minutes.

2. Add the beef, pork and seasoning, and continue to cook for 5 minutes, then add the water and simmer for 30 minutes.

3. Add the potatoes and macaroni and cook for a further 30 minutes, adjusting the seasoning, if necessary, before serving.

Not suitable for freezing.

Can be prepared in advance until 3.

Hot

Brewer's Stew

450 g. (1 lb.) braising steak
450 g. (1 lb.) fillet of pork
3 large red peppers
450 g. (1 lb.) small button onions

335 g. ($\frac{3}{4}$ lb.) button mushrooms
3 tablespoons oil
9 dl. (1$\frac{1}{2}$ pints) bitter beer
seasoned flour (p. 198)
seasoning

Preparation

Cut the fat off the meat and cut into bite-size pieces, keeping the beef and pork separate. Wash, deseed and chop the peppers. Skin the onions. Wash the mushrooms. Toss the meat in the seasoned flour.

Action

1. Sauté the peppers and beef in the oil in a large covered saucepan for 10 minutes. Add the beer and continue to cook for a further 15 minutes.

2. Add the pork, onions and mushrooms. Season and cook for a further 45 minutes.

Suitable for freezing.

Can be prepared in advance.

135

Hot

Hunter's Pork

1 kg. (2¼ lb.) boned loin of
    pork
670 g. (1½ lb.) Jerusalem
    artichokes
220 g. (½ lb.) mushrooms
220 g. (½ lb.) young carrots

6 dl. (1 pint) bitter beer
1 teaspoon lemon juice
1 sprig rosemary
¼ teaspoon chilli powder
seasoning

Preparation

Slice the pork into six to eight pieces. Peel the artichokes and cut
the large ones in half. Wash and slice the mushrooms and carrots.

Action

1. Place the pork in your grilling tray so that the fat is raised to
   the heat. Sprinkle with lemon juice, chilli powder, plenty of
   black pepper and salt. Put under a hot fire until the fat turns
   brown.
2. Allow the meat to cool and pour away the liquid fat which will
   have run out of the meat. Cut the meat into bite-size pieces,
   discarding any small bits of bone or gristle which may still be
   attached to the bottom of the meat.
3. Put the meat in a casserole together with the vegetables, and
   rosemary. Season, and pour in the beer. Cover and place in a
   moderate oven for 2 hours.

Suitable for freezing.

Can be prepared in advance.

Hot

Okra Pork

1 kg. (2¼ lb.) boned loin of
    pork
½ kg. (1 lb. 2 oz.) okra
220 g. (½ lb.) leeks
6 dl. (1 pint) water

1 teaspoon vegetable extract
1 teaspoon lemon juice
¼ teaspoon chilli powder
seasoning

Preparation

Slice the pork into six to eight pieces. Cut the tops off the okra and slice in half. Thoroughly wash and trim the leeks, removing the dark green parts, then slice the white parts.

Action

1. Place the pork in your grilling tray so that the fat is raised to the heat. Sprinkle with the lemon juice, chilli powder, plenty of black pepper, and salt. Put under a hot fire until the fat turns dark brown.

2. Allow the meat to cool and pour away the liquid fat which will have run out of the meat. Cut the meat into bite-size pieces, discarding any small pieces of bone or gristle which may still be attached to the bottom of the meat.

3. Boil the water and dissolve the vegetable extract, then put the meat, okra and leeks into a casserole, adjust seasoning and cover with the water and the dissolved vegetable extract. Cover and place in a moderate oven for $1\frac{1}{4}$ hours.

Suitable for freezing.

Can be prepared in advance.

Hot

Chinese Pork

$\frac{3}{4}$ kg. (1 lb. 11 oz.) slices belly of pork

2 onions

$\frac{1}{4}$ kg. (9 oz.) button mushrooms

140 g. (5 oz.) water chestnuts

$\frac{1}{2}$ kg. (1 lb. 2 oz.) bean shoots

$1\frac{1}{2}$ dl. ($\frac{1}{4}$ pint) tomato purée

$1\frac{1}{2}$ dl. ($\frac{1}{4}$ pint) malt vinegar

$1\frac{1}{2}$ dl. ($\frac{1}{4}$ pint) soy sauce

$1\frac{1}{2}$ dl. ($\frac{1}{4}$ pint) (approx.) stock (p. 198)

110 g. ($\frac{1}{4}$ lb.) moist brown sugar

lemon pepper

salt

a knob of butter

oil if necessary (see recipe)

$\frac{1}{2}$ kg. (1 lb. 2 oz.) noodles

Preparation

Cut the rind and any bits of bone from the pork and cut into short slices across the grain the width of a 10p. piece. Peel and slice the onions. Wash and slice the mushrooms. Slice the water chestnuts. Wash the bean shoots.

Action

1. Brown the belly of pork in its own fat in a large frying-pan. Add the onions, adding a minimum amount of oil if necessary, and brown.

2. Mix together the tomato purée, vinegar, soy sauce, stock and sugar. Pour over the meat and stir.

3. Add the mushrooms, water chestnuts, lemon pepper and salt. Cover and cook for 10 minutes over a gentle heat. Add more stock if the mixture appears too dry.

4. Put a pan of well salted water on to boil and cook the noodles in it for 10 minutes. Drain and toss with the knob of butter. Keep warm in a large dish.

5. Add the bean shoots to the meat mixture. Stir well, cover and cook for 5 minutes.

6. Serve surrounded by the noodles.

Not suitable for freezing.

Not suitable for advance preparation.

Hot

Fillet of Pork with Tagliatelle

¾ kg. (1 lb. 11 oz.) pork fillet
335 g. (¾ lb.) mushrooms
4 large tomatoes
85 g. (3 oz.) butter
1½ dl. (¼ pint) white wine
2 dl. (⅓ pint) commercially
    soured cream

1 tablespoon lemon juice
1 teaspoon tarragon (fresh if
    possible)
seasoned flour (p. 198)
seasoning
½ kg. (1 lb. 2 oz.) tagliatelle
    verdi

138

Preparation

Cut the pork fillet into thin strips about 3·75 cm. (1½ in.) long. Wash and slice the mushrooms. Peel and very finely chop the tomatoes. Coat the meat well with the seasoned flour.

Action

1. Heat the butter in a heavy pan, preferably one which will go into the oven as well as on top of the cooker. Add the meat and mushrooms. Sprinkle over the lemon juice, tarragon and seasoning. Cook for 15 minutes over a low heat, stirring regularly.

2. Blend in the wine and tomatoes. Cover the dish and transfer to a low oven for 30 minutes.

3. Crush the tagliatelle balls lightly to make it more manageable to eat, then cook for 5 minutes in plenty of fast-boiling salted water. Drain and arrange in a large serving dish.

4. At the point of service, take the dish from the oven and stir in the sour cream. Adjust the seasoning, and pour into the centre of the dish of tagliatelle.

Not suitable for freezing.

Can be prepared in advance until 3.

Cold

Meat and Vegetable Salad

½ kg. (1 lb. 2 oz.) pork fillet	60 g. (2 oz.) butter
½ kg. (1 lb. 2 oz.) lean lamb or beef	3 dl. (½ pint) commercially soured cream
½ onion	2 bayleaves
3 spring onions	¼ teaspoon thyme
½ kg. (1 lb. 2 oz.) tomatoes	seasoning
½ cucumber	lettuce
½ small green pepper	chopped parsley for garnishing
110 g. (¼ lb.) button mushrooms	

Preparation

Cut the meat into bite-size pieces, discarding any fat or gristle. Skin and rough chop the onion. Skin and finely chop the white part of the spring onions. Peel and chop all but three of the tomatoes which you should reserve for garnishing. Wash and slice the mushrooms. Peel and dice the cucumber. Wash, deseed and dice the pepper.

Action

1. Heat the butter in a frying-pan and cook the meat, together with the onion, bayleaves, thyme and seasoning, for 7–15 minutes, depending on your taste, turning frequently.

2. When the meat is cooked, take it from the pan with the onion and discard the bayleaves, then leave to cool.

3. When cold, mix the meat with all the chopped vegetables. Stir in the sour cream and season carefully. Chill until required.

4. Serve on a bed of lettuce and garnish with slices of the reserved tomatoes, and sprinkle liberally with freshly chopped parsley.

Not suitable for freezing.

Can be prepared in advance until 3.

Hot

Bacon and Chicken Moussaka

670 g. (1½ lb.) cold cooked bacon joint	85 g. (3 oz.) fresh white breadcrumbs
½ medium-sized cold roast chicken	6 tablespoons oil
335 g. (¾ lb.) soft fat cheese	110 g. (4 oz.) butter
2 large onions	60 g. (2 oz.) flour
½ kg. (1 lb. 2 oz.) tomatoes	6 dl. (1 pint) milk
2 large aubergines	3 dl. (½ pint) bitter beer
	6 drops Worcester sauce
	seasoning

Preparation

Remove the fat from the bacon and mince the meat. Remove the

140

skin and bone from the chicken and discard, then mince the meat.
Grate the cheese. Peel and chop the onions and tomatoes. Wash
and top and tail the aubergines, and thinly slice.

Action

1. Cook the onions in 2 tablespoons of the oil in a covered pan
   for 5 minutes, until they are soft but not brown. Add the minced
   bacon and chicken and the tomatoes. Season. Add the Worcester sauce and beer. Cover and cook very gently for 1 hour.

2. Meanwhile sauté the aubergine slices in the rest of the oil until
   they are soft.

3. Make a white sauce (p. 203) with three-quarters of the butter,
   the flour and the milk. When the sauce has boiled for 4
   minutes, stir in all but 2 tablespoons of the cheese.

4. When the meat has cooked, butter a pie-dish with the remaining butter and sprinkle over a third of the breadcrumbs. On
   top of this spread a layer of aubergine, then some of the meat
   mixture, alternately until both are used up. Pour the cheese
   sauce on top and finish with the rest of the breadcrumbs and
   the remaining grated cheese. Place in a moderate oven for 40
   minutes.

Suitable for freezing.

Can be prepared in advance.

Cold

Jellied Peach and Ham

¾ kg. (1 lb. 11 oz.) cooked
  ham, thickly sliced
4 large ripe peaches
9 dl. (1½ pints) aspic (p. 199)

2 tablespoons redcurrant jelly
1 dessertspoon Worcester
  sauce

Preparation

Dice the ham. Skin the peaches by plunging them for 1 minute
into boiling water, then immediately into cold water.

141

Action

1. Make the aspic jelly, following the directions on the packet. Stir in the redcurrant jelly, until it is dissolved, and the Worcester sauce. Cool as quickly as possible, and just as it is beginning to set spoon a little into a dish from which you will ultimately be able to turn it.

2. Place a layer of ham on the aspic. Slice the peaches and add a layer of them on top. Spoon over another layer of aspic and put it for 5 minutes in the ice compartment of the refrigerator or in the deep freeze so that it sets quickly. Continue in this manner until all the ingredients are used up. Chill in the refrigerator until you are ready to serve it, at which point you should turn the jelly out on to a plate, possibly on a bed of lettuce, or otherwise attractively garnished (p. 199).

Not suitable for freezing.

Can be prepared in advance.

Cold

Ham Mousse

¾ kg. (1 lb. 11 oz.) ham or gammon	1 420 g. (15 oz.) tin consommé
4 eggs	1 dl. (⅙ pint) white wine
1 large onion	1½ dl. (¼ pint) double cream
4 carrots	1 tablespoon gelatin
110 g. (¼ lb.) butter	4 cloves
110 g. (¼ lb.) flour	a few peppercorns
4½ dl. (¾ pint) milk	seasoning

Preparation

Separate the eggs. Peel the onion and stud it with the cloves. Scrape the carrots.

Action

1. Put the ham joint in a large saucepan with the onion, carrots, peppercorns and sufficient water to cover. Cover, bring to the boil and simmer gently for 40 minutes.

2. Heat the consommé and dissolve the gelatin in it. Pour 2 dl. (⅓ pint) into a separate dish for use later as a glaze. Leave it all to cool.

3. Make a white sauce with the butter, flour, milk and unreserved consommé (p. 203). Boil for 5 minutes.

4. Remove the pan from the heat and mix a little of the sauce with the egg yolks, then tip the egg yolks into the sauce, together with the wine and seasoning. Make sure the sauce is not too hot or it will scramble the egg. Mix well and leave to cool.

5. When the ham is cooked, mince it, discarding the other contents of the pan, then place with the sauce in a blender or Mouli and mix until smooth.

6. When the mixture from the blender is cool, stir in the cream. Stiffly beat the egg whites and fold in. Adjust the seasoning. Pour into a soufflé dish and leave to set in the refrigerator.

7. When the mousse has set, garnish with perhaps strips of cucumber peel and tomatoes to look like flowers. Spoon over the reserved consommé. It will probably be necessary to heat it again slightly, then to cool it to get the right consistency, which is when it is *just* beginning to set.

Suitable for freezing.

Can be prepared in advance.

Hot

Smoked Sausage with Rösti

1¼ kg. (2¾ lb.) large potatoes	8 tablespoons oil
4 220 g. (½ lb.) smoked pork sausages	seasoning

Preparation

Scrub the potatoes, but do not peel.

Action

1. Boil the potatoes in their skins in the normal way. When

K   143

cooked drain and allow to get cold, then skin. Grate the potatoes on the largest bit of your cheese grater. Season them.

2. Heat the oil in two large frying-pans since you don't want the potatoes to be too thick. When the oil is hot, press the potatoes down into the pan and cook loosening the edges as you would making an omelette, until one side is brown. This takes 10 minutes approximately. Carefully turn the potato in one piece by turning into a plate that fits the pan, then gently slide back into the frying-pan with the browned side uppermost. Add a little more oil to the pan if necessary before cooking the second side in a similar way to the first.

3. While the potato is cooking, boil the sausages in their bags for 15 minutes as directed on the packet. When cooked, peel off the skin and cut into slices.

4. Put the rösti on to a plate and arrange the slices of sausage around it.

Not suitable for freezing, although the sausages may be frozen.

Not suitable for advance preparation.

Note: Rösti can be used as the base of a number of supper dishes, and it is particularly good served with fried eggs and/or bacon.

Hot
Sausage and Apple Casserole

1 kg. (2¼ lb.) boiling ring sausage	3 tablespoons oil
8 onions	1 tablespoon French mustard
3 cooking apples	3 tablespoons castor sugar
½ kg. (1 lb. 2 oz.) tomatoes	seasoning

Preparation

Skin the boiling ring and cut the sausage into slices about 6 mm (¼ in.) thick. Peel and slice the onions and tomatoes. Peel and core the apples and slice.

144

Action

1. Heat the oil in a frying-pan and sauté the onions for 10 minutes until soft but not brown.

2. Put a layer of the onions in the bottom of a large casserole. Cover with a layer of sausage, on which you should spread some mustard. Follow this with an apple layer, over which you should sprinkle a little sugar, then a tomato layer covered with seasoning. Repeat the layers until all the ingredients are used up.

3. Cover the casserole and bake in a moderate oven for 1 hour.

Suitable for freezing.

Can be prepared in advance.

Hot

Aubergine Kidneys

1 kg. (2¼ lb.) ox kidney
2 onions
2 220 g. (½ lb.) tins mixed
   aubergines, peppers and
   tomatoes
3 tablespoons oil

1½ dl. (¼ pint) red wine or
   stock (p. 198)
¼ teaspoon basil
seasoned flour (p. 198)
seasoning

Preparation

Cut the kidneys from the core into bite-size pieces, and coat with the seasoned flour. Peel and slice the onions.

Action

1. Heat the oil in a frying-pan, or in a casserole which can go both on top of the stove and in the oven. Add the onions. Cook gently for 10 minutes, then add the kidneys and cook for 7 minutes, turning regularly, so that each piece is sealed.

2. Add the tins of vegetables, wine or stock, basil and seasoning. Stir until the mixture begins to bubble. Transfer to a casserole if necessary, and cook in a slow oven for 1 hour.

Suitable for freezing.

Can be prepared in advance.

Note: This dish uses the tinned ratatouille for reasons of economy, but if you prefer to make your own use the recipe on p. 71, but leave out the courgettes, and cut down a little on the onions.

Hot

Two Mustard Kidneys

20 lambs' kidneys	1½ tablespoons French
4 onions	mustard
3 tablespoons oil	1½ teaspoons dry English
3 dl. (½ pint) bitter beer or	mustard
pale ale	½ teaspoon lemon pepper
4 dl. (⅔ pint) double cream	seasoning

Preparation

Skin the kidneys and remove the cores, then cut each into about six pieces. Peel and chop the onions. Mix the mustards with the beer.

Action

1. Sauté the onions in the oil in a covered pan for 10 minutes. Add the kidneys and cook for a further 15 minutes.
2. Add the lemon pepper and the beer mixture. Season, and simmer for 5 minutes.
3. Stir in the cream just before serving. Heat, but do not boil. Adjust seasoning.

Not suitable for freezing.

Not suitable for advance preparation.

Hot

Tongue with Radishes

1 fresh medium-sized ox	60 g. (2 oz.) butter
tongue	9 dl. (1½ pints) water
450 g. (1 lb.) leeks	2 teaspoons arrowroot
2 bunches radishes	seasoning

Preparation

Thoroughly wash and trim the leeks, removing the dark green part, and slice the white parts. Wash the radishes and top and tail them.

Action

1. Simmer the tongue in two-thirds of the water for 1 hour. Strain the juice into a jug and lift the tongue out of the pan. The skin will now be slightly loosened, and you should remove it with a sharp knife. Cut the tongue into bite-size pieces, discarding any fat or gristle.
2. Simmer the leeks in the butter in a covered pan for 10 minutes so that they are soft but not brown. Add the rest of the water and the radishes, and continue to simmer for a further 10 minutes.
3. Mix the arrowroot with half the juice from the tongue and heat until it thickens. Add this, together with the tongue, to the vegetables. Season. Cover and simmer for a further 2½ hours. Adjust seasoning before serving.

Not suitable for freezing.

Can be prepared in advance.

Hot

Sweetbreads with Crab Sauce

1¾ kg. (4 lb.) lambs' sweetbreads
220 g. (½ lb.) brown and white
  crabmeat
4 tomatoes

60 g. (2 oz.) butter
2 dl. (⅓ pint) white wine
3 dl. (½ pint) double cream
2 tablespoons chopped parsley
seasoning

Preparation

Remove any fat from the sweetbreads. Peel and chop the tomatoes.

Action

1. Simmer the crab, tomatoes, wine, parsley and seasoning in a covered pan for 5 minutes.

2. Tip the contents of the pan into a blender or put through a Mouli. Adjust seasoning and return to the pan.

3. Sauté the sweetbreads in the butter over a moderate heat for 15 minutes. Drain off the juice which will have resulted. Season the sweetbreads, using lots of freshly ground black pepper.

4. Heat the crab sauce, and when hot stir in the cream. Warm but do not boil. Place the sweetbreads in a serving dish and pour over the sauce.

Not suitable for freezing.

Can be prepared a few hours in advance if reheated very gently in the oven.

Hot

Frito Misto

8 sets of lambs' brains	110 g. (¼ lb.) flour
450 g. (1 lb.) chicken livers	1½ dl. (¼ pint) of a mixture of
450 g. (1 lb.) sweetbreads	milk and water
85 g. (3 oz.) mild English	seasoned flour
cheese	seasoning
195 g. (7 oz.) olives stuffed	6 dl. (1 pint) oil for deep
with anchovies	frying
1 egg	lemons

Preparation

Wash the brains and cut each set into 6 to 8 pieces. Remove any skin or fat from the chicken livers and sweetbreads. Grate the cheese.

Action

1. Make a heavy batter, breaking the egg into the flour, mixing it well in and then stirring in the milk and water and beating well. Season.

2. Heat the oil in a deep frying-pan. Put the seasoned flour in a bag and add the brains, shaking well. Place the brains in the

148

frying basket and place this in the hot oil. Fry until golden, about 4 minutes.

3. When the brains are cooking, shake the chicken livers in the seasoned flour. Transfer the brains to a fire-proof serving dish and put in the oven to keep hot. Fry the chicken livers in the oil and put them in the oven on a second fire-proof dish.

4. While the chicken livers are cooking, roll the sweetbreads in the batter and fry them in the same way, transferring them to the oven.

5. Finally add the cheese to the remains of the batter mixture and roll the olives in this. Fry like the others. Mix all the ingredients together and serve with plenty of fresh lemon.

Not suitable for freezing.

Not suitable for advance preparation.

Hot

Lasagne Robinson

¼ kg. (9 oz.) lasagne pasta	¾ kg. (1 lb. 11 oz.) tinned
½ kg. (1 lb. 2 oz.) sausage	Italian plum tomatoes
meat	220 g. (½ lb.) tomato purée
670 g. (1½ lb.) ricotta cheese	1½ dl. (¼ pint) commercially
85 g. (3 oz.) grated Parmesan	soured cream
cheese	4 tablespoons chopped parsley
220 g. (½ lb.) mozzarella	3 tablespoons (approx.) oil
cheese	seasoning
3 cloves garlic	

Preparation

Mix together the ricotta cheese, sour cream and parsley. Cut the mozzarella cheese into strips. Peel and finely chop or crush the garlic.

Action

1. Fill two large shallow pans (we use frying-pans) with well salted water, to each of which you should add a little oil,

149

and bring to the boil. Cook the lasagne leaves, three or four at a time, in the water for 11 minutes, stirring from time to time to stop them sticking together. They are devilish at this, which is why you have to go through the laborious business of doing a few at a time. Keep the water, salt and oil topped up until you have finished cooking them all. As the leaves are cooked, lift them individually from the pan with a slice, and lay separately on a clean tea towel to drain.

2. Meanwhile, brown the sausage meat in a large saucepan in its own fat, with the garlic.

3. Mix the tomatoes and tomato purée with the sausage meat, season well and simmer gently for 15 minutes. If the sauce thickens too much, add 1½ dl. (¼ pint) water, but this probably won't be necessary.

4. When both the pasta and the sauce are cooked, grease a large square heat-proof dish and put in it alternate layers of the tomato and meat mixture, the lasagne, and the ricotta cheese mixture, repeating until they are all used up.

5. Spread the mozzarella cheese over the top of the dish, then sprinkle over the Parmesan.

6. Cook in a moderate oven for 45 minutes, or until the cheese is really bubbling.

Suitable for freezing.

Can be prepared in advance until 6.

Hot

Roquefort Macaroni

450 g. (1 lb.) large macaroni
220 g. (½ lb.) Roquefort cheese
450 g. (1 lb.) mozzarella
  cheese
4½ dl. (¾ pint) milk

2 dl. (⅓ pint) single cream
1 teaspoon salt
½ teaspoon paprika
seasoning

Preparation

Grate or finely chop the cheeses and mix together.

Action

1. Boil the macaroni with the salt and plenty of water for about 13 minutes, or until soft. Drain in a colander and run under cold water to cool.

2. Slit open about half the macaroni and fill with the cheese mixture. Place in a deep dish and spread the remains of the cheese and macaroni on top.

3. Pour over the milk and leave in the refrigerator for 24 hours.

4. Drain off the wey which will have formed.

5. Heat the macaroni slowly in a large saucepan, stirring carefully. Add the cream and seasoning, and place in a pre-heated serving dish. Dust with paprika.

Suitable for freezing at the end of stage 4.

Can be prepared in advance until 5.

Note: It may seem crazy to bother stuffing the macaroni when the cheese melts anyway and runs out, but the Roquefort leaves a deposit inside the macaroni, which is the highlight of this dish.

Hot

Asparagus Macaroni

450 g. (1 lb.) large macaroni
1 kg. (2¼ lb.) grass (sprew) asparagus

4½ dl. (¾ pint) milk
2 dl. (⅓ pint) double cream
seasoning

Preparation
Wash the asparagus.

Action

1. Boil a pan of salted water and cook the macaroni in it for 13 minutes. Drain in a colander and run under cold water to cool.

2. At the same time, put another pan of salted water to boil, and cook the asparagus at simmering point for 15 minutes. Drain and cut off the heads where the asparagus starts to get stringy.

151

3. Stuff about two-thirds of the macaroni with the asparagus heads, cutting the heads when they are too long.
4. Put the stuffed macaroni into a saucepan together with the remains of the asparagus and macaroni, and add the milk and seasoning. Heat to simmering point, remove from the fire and stir in the cream. Warm, but do not boil.

Suitable for freezing, before adding the cream.

Can be prepared a few hours in advance until 4.

Hot

Bow Bell Macaroni

¼ kg. (9 oz.) bow tie macaroni
670 g. (1½ lb.) fresh minced beef
110 g. (¼ lb.) cottage cheese
110 g. (¼ lb.) mild English cheese
2 onions
¼ kg. (9 oz.) tomatoes
1 clove garlic

110 g. (¼ lb.) frozen chopped spinach
85 g. (3 oz.) butter
1 level tablespoon flour
2 dl. (⅓ pint) stock (p. 198)
2 dl. (⅓ pint) commercially soured cream
⅛ teaspoon grated nutmeg
¼ teaspoon tarragon seasoning

Preparation

Grate the hard cheese. Peel and chop the onions and tomatoes. Peel and very finely chop or squeeze the garlic. Leave the spinach to defrost.

Action

1. Heat two-thirds of the butter in a saucepan. Add the onions and cook for 10 minutes, then sprinkle over the flour. Gradually blend in the stock, tomatoes, tarragon and seasoning. Bring to the boil, cover the pan and simmer for 10 minutes.
2. Heat the other third of the butter in a frying-pan and lightly cook the meat with the garlic and seasoning. When both the meat and the sauce are ready, mix them together.

3. Put a pan of salted water on to boil and cook the macaroni in it for 10 minutes. Drain.

4. Mix together the spinach, cottage cheese and sour cream and sprinkle over a little nutmeg.

5. Lightly butter a casserole and put a layer of macaroni on the bottom, followed by a meat layer, then a spinach and cottage cheese layer. Repeat these layers once, using up all the ingredients.

6. Sprinkle over the grated cheese and cook uncovered in a moderate oven for 40 minutes, browning the top under the grill at the last moment if necessary.

Suitable for freezing before stage 6.

Can be prepared in advance until 6.

Hot
Tagliatelle with Chicken Liver Sauce

½ kg. (1 lb. 2 oz.) tagliatelle
1 kg. (2¼ lb.) chicken livers
4 leeks
1 red pepper (see Preparation)
½ kg. (1 lb. 2 oz.) tomatoes
110 g. (¼ lb.) butter

3 dl. (½ pint) chicken stock
 (p. 199)
½ teaspoon basil
seasoned flour (p. 198)
seasoning

Preparation

Remove any skin or fat from the chicken livers and coat them well with the seasoned flour. Thoroughly wash and trim the leeks, removing the dark green part, then thinly slice the white parts. Wash, deseed and chop the pepper (green will do, if red is unavailable). Peel and chop the tomatoes.

Action

1. Heat the butter in a heavy frying-pan and cook the leeks and pepper for 10 minutes over a low heat, stirring occasionally, but covering the pan meanwhile.

2. Add the chicken livers and basil and cook for 7 minutes with the pan uncovered.

3. Add the tomatoes and blend in the stock. Season well. Cover the pan and simmer gently for a further 10 minutes.

4. At the same time as you do stage 3, put a pan of well salted water on to boil. Lightly crush the tagliatelle balls before cooking for ease of eating, then cook for 7 minutes in the fast-boiling water, stirring occasionally. Drain and toss with a little butter to prevent the tagliatelle sticking together. Serve immediately with the sauce.

The sauce may be frozen, but pointless to freeze the tagliatelle.

Can be prepared in advance until 4.

Hot

Marrow Cheese

1 large but young marrow	450 g. (1 lb.) tomatoes
335 g. (¾ lb.) soft fat cheese	5 cloves garlic
3 onions	4 tablespoons oil
2 green peppers	1 teaspoon basil
2 aubergines	seasoning
335 g. (¾ lb.) courgettes	

Preparation

Peel the marrow and cut in half lengthwise. Scoop out the seeds, then cut each half into four pieces. Thinly slice the cheese. Peel and chop the onions and garlic. Wash, deseed and chop the peppers. Wash, top and tail, and chop the courgettes and aubergines. Peel and slice the tomatoes.

Action

1. Put the oil, onions and peppers in a covered pan and simmer for 10 minutes. Add the aubergines and continue to cook for 5 minutes. Add the courgettes, tomatoes, garlic, basil and seasoning, and continue to cook for a further 40 minutes.

2. Simmer the marrow in salted water for 10 minutes. Drain.

3. Arrange the marrow like boats in a fire-proof dish. Fill the boats with the ratatouille and cover with the cheese, adjusting the seasoning if necessary.

154

4. Bake in a hot oven for 25 minutes, or until the cheese has melted and browned.

The ratatouille may be frozen, but not the marrow, as it has to remain firm.

Can be prepared in advance until 4.

AFTERS

Hot

Omelette Surprise

12 eggs
2 tablespoons castor sugar
¼ kg. (9 oz.) unsalted butter*

8 dessertspoons jam
8 tablespoons icecream

Preparation

Divide the icecream and return to freezer or very cold refrigerator.

Action

1. Beat the eggs until frothy, then beat in the sugar.

2. Using 2 omelette pans, melt a quarter of the butter into each and then add a quarter of the beaten egg. When the omelette is firm, add 2 dessertspoons jam and 2 tablespoons icecream carefully, so that you can divide the omelette in half and give each person the same amount of jam and icecream.

3. Repeat the process, but don't let the cooked omelettes wait around. They must be eaten immediately.

Not suitable for freezing.

Not suitable for advance preparation.

Notes: It is *essential* to use unsalted butter for this recipe.

Plum jam with vanilla icecream is probably the best combination, but obviously you can combine a number of different flavours.

Cold

Éclairs

For the Choux Pastry
85 g. (3 oz.) butter
110 g. (4 oz.) plain flour
3 eggs
2 dl. (⅓ pint) water

For the Filling
3 dl. (½ pint) double cream

For the Icing
110 g. (¼ lb.) icing sugar
60 g. (2 oz.) bitter chocolate
¾ dl. (⅛ pint) water

1 teaspoon lard for greasing
   baking-tray

L   159

Preparation

Grease a baking-tray. Lightly beat the eggs. Sift the flour and icing sugar.

Action: Choux Pastry

1. Heat the butter and water together in a saucepan large enough to hold all the pastry ingredients, bring to the boil, then take the pan off the heat and *immediately* tip in all the flour. Beat with a wooden spoon only until the mixture cleanly leaves the side of the pan—be careful not to over-beat at this stage. Leave to cool.

2. Gradually add the beaten eggs to the paste when it has cooled. Beat the eggs in thoroughly with a wooden spoon. The paste should look shiny and smooth when you have finished this stage.

3. Put the paste into a forcing bag with a plain nozzle and pipe the mixture on to the baking-tray. Each piece should be about 4 cm. (1½ in.) long and well spaced out to allow for rising. Cook in a hot oven for 30 minutes or until they are quite firm to the touch. On no account take them out too early, or they will collapse. When cooked, slit in half and with a teaspoon scrape out any wet paste left in the middle, then leave to cool on a cake rack.

To Complete

4. Stiffly whip the cream, and when the éclairs are quite cold put an equal amount of cream in each and sandwich together again.

5. Make the icing by dissolving the chocolate over a gentle heat in the water. Remove from the heat. Pour the chocolate on to the icing sugar and mix well. When slightly cool, but still just warm, ice the éclairs. Chill until required.

Suitable for freezing.

Can be prepared in advance.

Cold

Iced Orange Cake

For the Cake
110 g. ($\frac{1}{4}$ lb.) butter
200 g. (7 oz.) castor sugar
grated rind of 2 oranges
4 eggs
220 g. ($\frac{1}{2}$ lb.) self-raising flour
1$\frac{1}{2}$ dl. ($\frac{1}{4}$ pint) milk
1 teaspoon cream of tartar

For the Icing
$\frac{1}{2}$ kg. (1 lb. 2 oz.) icing sugar
170 g. (6 oz.) butter
juice of 2 oranges
$\frac{1}{4}$ teaspoon lemon colouring

Preparation

Separate the eggs. Soften the butter, using a little to grease a 18 cm. (7 in.) cake tin. Sieve the icing sugar and the flour.

Action: Cake

1. Beat the butter until it is light and creamy, then add the sugar and orange peel. Beat well.

2. Add the egg yolks, then the flour, alternating it with splashes of the milk until both are used up. Beat in the cream of tartar.

3. Whisk the egg whites and fold into the mixture. Pour into the cake tin and bake in a slow oven for 1$\frac{1}{2}$ hours. Turn out on to a cake rack and cool.

Action: Icing

4. Beat the butter until light and creamy, and beat in 200 g. (7 oz.) of the icing sugar, which should first be mixed with two-thirds of the orange juice.

5. Cut the cake in half and fill with the orange butter icing.

6. Put the rest of the icing sugar, the lemon colouring and the remaining third of the orange juice into a saucepan and stir until you have the consistency of a thick sauce.

7. Place the cake sideways in a bowl large enough to take it, propped up on either side by two cups to keep it from touching

the bottom. Pour the icing sugar over the exposed side, turning like a wheel twice so that the whole of the side of the cake is covered. The icing will have to be reheated between each motion. Finally, carefully place the cake the right way up on a plate and ice the top.

Not suitable for freezing.

Can be prepared in advance, but the orange will run out of the butter icing after 24 hours, which spoils the look of the cake.

Cold

Sachertorte

For the Cake
45 g. (1½ oz.) unsalted butter
110 g. (¼ lb) castor sugar
4 eggs
110 g. (¼ lb.) bitter chocolate
30 g. (1 oz.) ground almonds
pinch salt

For the Filling
3 dl. (½ pint) double cream
2 tablespoons castor sugar
3 drops vanilla essence
3 tablespoons apricot jam
16 blanched almonds

Preparation

Line two 20 cm. (8 in.) sandwich tins with greaseproof paper. This is important for lifting out the delicate cakes after cooking. Separate 3 of the eggs.

Action: Cake

1. Cream together the butter, sugar and salt until light and smooth.

2. Beat in the egg yolks and the whole egg.

3. Melt the chocolate in a bowl over a pan of very hot water, and when smooth stir in the ground almonds.

4. Beat the chocolate mixture thoroughly into the other mixture.

5. Whip the egg whites until stiff and fold into the mixture. Divide mixture in half and pour into the prepared tins, and cook in a very moderate oven for 20 minutes.

Action: Filling

6. Stiffly whip the cream with the sugar and vanilla essence, then mix with the apricot jam.

7. When the cakes are cooked, take them from the oven and allow to cool in their tins (about 30 minutes), then very carefully lift them out and peel off the greaseproof paper.

8. Put the two halves together, using two-thirds of the cream mixture as a filler. Smooth the rest of the cream over the top, then decorate with the blanched almonds, and possibly a little grated chocolate. Chill until required.

Not suitable for freezing.

Can be prepared in advance, but the cream 'icing' tends to discolour after a few hours, so it is better to leave this until an hour or two before you are ready to eat.

Note: The traditional sachertorte is iced with chocolate butter icing, but we feel this is just too rich.

Hot or Cold

Apple Flan

4 large Cox's Orange Pippin apples	$\frac{1}{2}$ teaspoon cinnamon
3 tablespoons apricot jam	$\frac{1}{4}$ kg. (9 oz.) shortcrust pastry (p. 195) plus 1 tablespoon
2 tablespoons water	icing sugar (see recipe)

Preparation

Nil.

Action

1. Make the pastry, adding the icing sugar to the rubbed-in mixture. Roll out to line a 23–25 cm. (9–10 in.) flan case and bake blind for 15 minutes. Cool.

2. Heat the apricot jam with the water and keep warm.

3. When the pastry is cool, sprinkle the cinnamon over it.

4. Peel, core and slice the apples and lay out in an attractive pattern over the pastry.

5. Strain the apricot jam evenly over the apples.

6. Return the flan to a moderate oven for 15 minutes. Serve hot or cold with cream.

Not suitable for freezing.

Can be prepared in advance.

Cold

Blackcurrant Shortcrust

¼ kg. (9 oz.) blackcurrants
110 g. (¼ lb.) granulated sugar
220 g. (½ lb.) Philadelphia
  cheese
1½ dl. (¼ pint) commercially
  soured cream
4 tablespoons water
1 dessertspoon arrowroot

For the Pastry
140 g. (5 oz.) flour
60 g. (3 oz.) butter
2 tablespoons castor sugar
1 egg yolk

Preparation
Nil.

Action

1. Sift the flour into a bowl with the salt. Add the butter in small pieces and rub in. When well rubbed in, add the castor sugar and bind together with the egg yolk. Roll into a ball on a well floured board, then press out in a 23–25 cm. (9–10 in.) flan tin to cover the bottom. Prick with a fork and cook in a pre-heated moderate oven for 30 minutes. Turn out and cool.

2. Meanwhile, gently cook the blackcurrants with half the water and the granulated sugar. Mix the arrowroot with the rest of the water, and when the fruit is soft, stir it in and boil for 2 minutes. Withdraw the pan from the heat.

3. Mix together the cheese and sour cream.

4. When the shortcrust is quite cool, put it on a plate and spread with the cheese mixture. Spread the blackcurrants over this. Chill until required.

Not suitable for freezing.

Can be prepared in advance.

Cold

Cheese and Plum Flan

6 very ripe Victoria plums
170 g. (1½ lb.) Philadelphia
  cheese
3 lemons
110 g. (¼ lb.) castor sugar
2 eggs

For the Flan Base
85 g. (3 oz.) unsalted butter
170 g. (6 oz.) Rich Tea biscuits

Preparation

Crush the biscuits to crumbs in a polythene bag, with a rolling pin. Wash and stone the plums and cut each into about six pieces. Grate the rind from the lemons and squeeze the juice. Separate the egg.

Action

1. Melt the butter and pour it over the crumbs and mix well together. Press this mixture into a 23–25 cm. (9–10 in.) flan case to act as a lining. Put to set in the refrigerator for at least 1 hour.

2. Mix together until smooth the cheese, lemon juice and rind, sugar and egg yolk.

3. Stir in the pieces of plum, and finally whip the egg white and fold in. Add more sugar to taste if necessary.

4. Spoon the mixture into the flan shell and set for a minimum of 3 hours in the refrigerator.

Not suitable for freezing.

Can be prepared in advance.

Cold

Hilary's Farewell Flan

4 peaches
170 g. (6 oz.) raspberries
110 g. (¼ lb.) castor sugar
1½ dl. (¼ pint) water
3 dl. (½ pint) white wine
1 tablespoon gelatin

For the Flan Base
85 g. (3 oz.) butter
170 g. (6 oz.) Nice biscuits

Preparation

Crush the biscuits to crumbs in a polythene bag, with a rolling pin. Cool the wine in the refrigerator. Peel the peaches—the easiest method of doing this is to plunge the peaches into boiling water for 1 minute, then directly into cold water. Cut the peaches in half, reserving the skins and stones.

Action

1. Melt the butter and mix in the biscuits, then line a 23 cm. (9 in.) flan case with the mixture, and put to set in the refrigerator for 1–2 hours.

2. Put the peach stones and skin into a saucepan with the water and sugar. Cover and simmer gently for 10 minutes. Meanwhile, put the gelatin in a bowl with about 2 tablespoons of water and leave it to soak.

3. While the juice is simmering, slice the peaches thinly and arrange over the bottom of the flan in an attractive pattern. On top of these arrange the raspberries.

4. After 10 minutes, strain the juice into a bowl, discarding the skin and stones. Stir in the soaked gelatin until it is completely dissolved, then stir in the wine.

5. Put the flan and juice into the refrigerator separately until the juice begins to thicken—about 45 minutes if the wine was really cold before starting—then spoon the juice carefully over the top, taking care not to disturb the fruit. Return to the

refrigerator until the jelly is completely set, and leave there until needed.

Not suitable for freezing.

Can be prepared in advance.

Cold

Chocolate Tycoon

16 ginger nuts
8 tablespoons brandy with
   8 dessertspoons water
335 g. (¾ lb.) plain chocolate
1 dl. (⅙ pint) water
4 dl. (⅔ pint) double cream

For the Cake
6 eggs
170 g. (6 oz.) castor sugar
140 g. (5 oz.) flour
30 g. (1 oz.) butter for
   greasing tins

Preparation

Grease the sandwich tins with the butter.*

Action

1. Beat the eggs and sugar over a low heat until the mixture thickens, then, continuing to beat, sieve in the flour.
2. Pour the mixture into the sandwich tins and bake in a moderate oven for 25 minutes. Turn out on to a cake rack and cool.
3. Place a ginger nut at the base of each dessert bowl and crumble a second biscuit around it. Pour over the brandy and water.
4. Melt the chocolate with the water over a gentle heat.
5. Whip the cream and place on top of the biscuit. Cut the sponge into circles to fit in your glass dessert bowls on top of the cream, then pour the melted chocolate on top, taking care that it is not too hot or it will crack your bowls. Chill until required.

Not suitable for freezing.

Can be prepared in advance.

Note: It is best to arrange your dessert bowls in your sandwich tins, face down, before selecting those tins you are to use. Obviously you want to avoid wasting more than the minimum of sponge.

Cold

Oxbridge Cake

220 g. ($\frac{1}{2}$ lb.) Nice biscuits
170 g. (6 oz.) butter
170 g. (6 oz.) castor sugar
1 egg
1 egg yolk
110 g. ($\frac{1}{4}$ lb.) bitter chocolate

2 tablespoons water
1 tablespoon rum
1 dl. ($\frac{1}{6}$ pint) (approx.) coffee
 essence
60 g. (2 oz.) walnuts

Preparation
Chop the walnuts.

Action

1. Cream together the butter and sugar. Very gradually blend in the whole egg and the egg yolk.
2. Melt the chocolate with the water over a very gentle heat.
3. Beat the melted chocolate and the rum into the creamed mixture.
4. Put the coffee essence into a bowl and dip the biscuits in it, one at a time.
5. Spread the chocolate mixture on each biscuit and pile them together in a block 5 biscuits long, 1 biscuit wide and 4 biscuits tall. See that all the biscuits are well covered, then sprinkle with the chopped walnuts. Chill until required, and slice to serve.

Not suitable for freezing.

Can be prepared in advance.

Hot

Bread and Butter Pudding

10 slices white bread
85 g. (3 oz.) butter
4 tablespoons currants
3 tablespoons pickled
 watermelon rind*

4 eggs
1 litre (1$\frac{2}{3}$ pints) milk
60 g. (2 oz.) castor sugar

Preparation

Butter a pie-dish. Chop the watermelon rind. Cut the crusts from the bread.

Action

1. Butter the bread and place in the pie-dish in layers with the currants and watermelon rind in between. Top with a layer of bread.
2. Beat the eggs and then add the milk and sugar. Pour over the bread and place in a moderate oven for 25 minutes.

Not suitable for freezing.

Not suitable for advance preparation.

*Note: If you can't get this, you can make the pudding without it, using extra dried fruit.

Hot

Scandinavian Creamed Rice

6 tablespoons pudding (Carolina) rice	2 dl. ($\frac{1}{3}$ pint) milk
85 g. (3 oz.) castor sugar	6 eggs
	6 dl. (1 pint) double cream
	$\frac{1}{2}$ teaspoon vanilla essence

Preparation

Separate the eggs.

Action

1. Boil the rice in a large pan of water for 20 minutes.
2. Drain and add the sugar and milk, and when cool enough beat in the egg yolks and vanilla essence.
3. Return the pan to the heat while you beat the egg whites stiffly. Stir in the cream and then fold in the egg whites. Continue to heat, but do not allow to boil.

Not suitable for freezing.

Can be prepared in advance until 3.

Hot

Rice Meringues

3½ tablespoons pudding
   (Carolina) rice
9 dl. (1½ pints) milk
4 eggs

140 g. (5 oz.) castor sugar
¼ teaspoon vanilla essence
8 teaspoons blackcurrant jam

Preparation
Separate the eggs.

Action

1. Simmer the rice and milk in a saucepan for 20 minutes.
2. Cool slightly and beat in the egg yolks, a quarter of the sugar, and the vanilla essence.
3. Whisk the egg whites until stiff. Add all but 1 dessertspoon of the remaining sugar, and whisk again.
4. Put a teaspoon of jam in each of 8 ramekin dishes, spoon over the rice and top with the white of egg. Sprinkle over the rest of the sugar, and put the ramekins in a slow oven for 25 minutes.

Not suitable for freezing.

Not suitable for advance preparation.

Hot or cold

Rhubarb Crumble

1 kg. (2¼ lb.) rhubarb
¼ kg. (9 oz.) granulated sugar
170 g. (6 oz.) flour

85 g. (3 oz.) butter
4 tablespoons castor sugar
pinch salt

Preparation
Wash the rhubarb and cut into pieces about 2·5 cm. (1 in.) long.

Action

1. Sieve the flour into a mixing bowl with the salt. Add the butter

in small pieces. Rub together with your fingers until you have something the consistency of breadcrumbs. Stir in the castor sugar.

2. Put the rhubarb in a pie-dish with the granulated sugar. Sprinkle the crumble mixture on top of the rhubarb.

3. Cook in a hot oven for 35 minutes, and serve immediately, with cream, or cool and chill until required if eating cold.

Not suitable for freezing.

Not suitable for advance preparation, although the crumble can be made and kept separately but it will go soggy if left on the rhubarb.

Hot

Crunchy Apple

6 large cooking apples	110 g. ($\frac{1}{4}$ lb.) fresh white
1 large orange	breadcrumbs
85 g. (3 oz.) butter	3 tablespoons golden syrup
	$\frac{3}{4}$ teaspoon cinnamon

Preparation

Peel, core and slice the apples. Grate the rind from the orange and squeeze the juice.

Action

1. With half the butter, generously grease the bottom and sides of a fairly large fireproof dish.

2. Sprinkle about two-thirds of the breadcrumbs over the dish and shake it so that the crumbs are evenly coated over the bottom and sides.

3. Spoon the golden syrup over the bottom of the dish as evenly as possible.

4. Cover the syrup with slices of apple. Pour over the orange juice. Sprinkle over the orange rind and cinnamon.

5. Cover the apple with the other breadcrumbs and dot with the remaining butter.

171

6. Bake in a hot oven for 40 minutes, when it should be crisp. Serve with cream.

Not suitable for freezing.

Can be prepared until 6, a few hours in advance.

Hot
Coffee Brandy Soufflé

1 tablespoon strong instant coffee granules	85 g. (3 oz.) self-raising flour
	1½ dl. (¼ pint) milk
6 tablespoons brandy	4 tablespoons castor sugar
6 eggs	4 tablespoons boiling water
100 g. (3½ oz.) butter	

Preparation
Separate the eggs.

Action

1. Make a very thick white sauce with the butter, flour and milk (p. 203), but do not add any seasoning. When the sauce has cooked for 4 minutes, cool.
2. Beat the egg yolks until creamy and add to the sauce. Pour the boiling water over the instant coffee and add to the sauce, together with the sugar and brandy.
3. Whisk the egg whites until they are stiff, and blend half into the mixture, mixing well. Lightly fold in the other half. Pour into 8 ramekin dishes and place in a moderate oven for 15 minutes.

Not suitable for freezing.

Not suitable for advance preparation.

Hot
Orange Chocolate Soufflé

2 oranges	85 g. (3 oz.) butter
2 crystallized oranges	60 g. (2 oz.) self-raising flour
220 g. (½ lb.) plain chocolate	1½ dl. (¼ pint) milk
6 eggs	1 tablespoon castor sugar

172

Preparation

Separate the eggs. Grate and squeeze the oranges. Chop the crystallized oranges.

Action

1. Make a very thick white sauce with the butter, flour and milk (p. 203), but do not add any seasoning. When the sauce has cooked for 4 minutes, cool.
2. Beat the egg yolks until creamy and add to the sauce. Add the orange rind. Stir well so that it is evenly distributed.
3. Put the chocolate, sugar and orange juice into a saucepan and heat gently until the chocolate is melted, then add this to the sauce.
4. Whisk the egg whites until they are stiff, then blend half into the mixture, mixing well. Lightly fold in the other half.
5. Divide the crystallized orange between 8 ramekin dishes, pour in the mixture, and place in a moderate oven for 15 minutes.

Not suitable for freezing.

Not suitable for advance preparation.

Icecream—General Instructions

Home-made icecream is delicious, and can be made with almost any kind of fruit purée. It should be remembered that freezing does tend to lessen flavours and sweetening, so when preparing purées for this purpose, bear this in mind. If you have an icecream-maker, you will obviously use it for the recipes that follow, but our recipes are designed for those without this equipment, and in order to get an icecream with a good consistency, it is absolutely essential that you should beat, or crush with a fork, the mixture several times while it is freezing. (Freezing takes 4–6 hours on average.) This is more easily done if you freeze the icecream in shallow trays. We also find that a better consistency is achieved if icing sugar is used, rather than any other form of sweetening.

Most of the recipes that follow use a custard base. The ingredients for this are 4 egg yolks to 3 dl. ($\frac{1}{2}$ pint) milk, plus varying amounts of icing sugar, depending on the acid content of the fruit involved in the individual recipes. There are two exceptions. The first is the recipe for coffee icecream: in this case, it is not necessary to make a custard since no fruit is involved, which means that the risk of the milk curdling is obviated. The second exception is the cranberry and orange icecream, which uses no milk, but double cream. This method is equally satisfactory, but more expensive.

To make the custard

Place the egg yolks, milk and icing sugar in the top of a double saucepan, or in a bowl over a pan of hot water. Whisk over a gentle heat until the mixture thickens. Do not on any account allow the custard to boil as it will then separate.

Home-made icecream always tends to set more firmly than its commercial counterpart, so it is a good idea to take it out of the freezing compartment about half an hour before you want to eat it, to allow it to mellow.

Cold

Quince and Lime Icecream

2 quinces	195 g. (7 oz.) icing sugar
3 limes	3 dl. ($\frac{1}{2}$ pint) water
4 egg yolks	6 dl. (1 pint) single cream
3 dl. ($\frac{1}{2}$ pint) milk	

Preparation

Cut up the quinces and squeeze the limes.

Action

1. Using the egg yolks, the milk and three-quarters of the sugar, make a custard (see above). Cool.
2. Boil the quinces in the water with the remaining sugar for 15 minutes, in an open saucepan so that the liquid is reduced.

3. Rub the quince and juice through a sieve and then through a very fine sieve, since on the first occasion the juice and flesh will separate. Cool.

4. Add the quince purée to the custard and stir in the lime juice and cream. Pour into a freezing container.

5. Place in the coldest part of your refrigerator or in a freezer. Beat the icecream several times before it is completely frozen to break down the ice crystals.

Suitable for freezing.
Can be prepared in advance.

Cold

Chinese Gooseberry and Lemon Icecream

Chinese gooseberries	3 dl. (½ pint) milk
lemon	170 g. (6 oz.) icing sugar
egg yolks	6 dl. (1 pint) single cream

Preparation

Peel the Chinese gooseberries and sieve them. Squeeze the juice from the lemon.

Action

1. Make a custard with the egg yolks, milk and sugar (p. 174). Cool.

2. Add the fruit purée and lemon juice to the custard, then stir in the cream. Pour into a freezing container.

3. Place in the coldest part of your refrigerator or in the freezer. Beat the icecream several times before it is completely frozen to break down the ice crystals.

Suitable for freezing.
Can be prepared in advance.

Cold
Blackberry and Apple Icecream

220 g. (½ lb.) blackberries   170 g. (6 oz.) icing sugar
3 hard eating apples   2 dl. (⅓ pint) water
4 egg yolks   6 dl. (1 pint) single cream
3 dl. (½ pint) milk

Preparation
Peel the apples, then grate them.

Action
1. Using the egg yolks, the milk and all but 1 tablespoon of the sugar, make a custard (p. 174). Cool.
2. Boil the blackberries in an open saucepan with the water and reserved sugar for 5 minutes. Cool.
3. Mix the blackberries with the apple, then put in a blender or Mouli and afterwards through a sieve.
4. Add the fruit purée to the custard, and stir in the cream. Pour into a freezing container.
5. Place in the coldest part of your refrigerator or in the freezer. Beat the icecream several times before it is completely frozen to break down the ice crystals.

Suitable for freezing.
Can be prepared in advance.

Cold
Plum Icecream

450 g. (1 lb.) ripe eating plums   3 dl. (½ pint) water
4 egg yolks   6 dl. (1 pint) commercially
3 dl. (½ pint) milk   soured cream
140 g. (5 oz.) icing sugar

Preparation
Nil.

Action

1. Make a custard with the egg yolks, milk and sugar (p. 174). Cool.

2. Boil the plums in the water for 6 minutes. Sieve, retaining the juice. Cool.

3. Mix the fruit purée with the custard, and stir in the soured cream. Pour into a freezing container.

4. Place in the coldest part of your refrigerator or in the freezer. Beat the icecream several times before it is completely frozen to break down the ice crystals.

Suitable for freezing.

Can be prepared in advance.

Cold

Youngberry and Orange Icecream

670 g. (1½ lb.) frozen young-   3 dl. (½ pint) milk
   berries   170 g. (6 oz.) icing sugar
3 oranges   6 dl. (1 pint) single cream
4 egg yolks

Preparation

Defrost the youngberries and sieve. Squeeze the oranges.

Action

1. Make a custard with the egg yolks, milk and sugar (p. 174). Cool.

2. Add the youngberry purée and orange juice to the custard, then stir in the cream. Pour into a freezing container.

3. Place in the coldest part of your refrigerator or in the freezer. Beat the icecream several times before it is completely frozen to break down the ice crystals.

Suitable for freezing.

Can be prepared in advance.

Cold

Cranberry and Orange Icecream

¾ kg. (1 lb. 11 oz.) cranberries   2 tablespoons brandy
2 large oranges   (optional)
¼ kg. (9 oz.) icing sugar   4½ dl. (¾ pint) double cream
2 eggs

Preparation

Wash the cranberries. Very finely grate the rind from the oranges, then squeeze the juice. Separate the eggs.

Action

1. Place the cranberries, sugar, orange juice and rind in a saucepan and cook over a low heat for about 10 minutes, or until the cranberries are soft. When cooked remove from the heat and leave to cool.

2. When cold, stir in the egg yolks and brandy. Whip the cream until thick and stir in, and finally whip the egg whites until stiff and fold in.

3. Pour into a freezing container and put into the freezing compartment of the refrigerator or a freezer. Beat several times during freezing to break down the ice crystals.

Suitable for freezing.

Can be prepared in advance.

Cold

Camilla's Sundae

16 scoops quince and lime   8 teaspooons Vieille Curé
    icecream (p. 174)   liqueur
16 scoops blackberry and   12 tablespoons (approx.)
    apple icecream (p. 176)   maple syrup
16 scoops plum icecream (p.   4 dessertspoons chopped
    176)   almonds

Preparation
Nil.

Action

In each of eight sundae glasses, put a teaspoon of the Vieille Curé, followed by about 4 cm. (1½ in.) of maple syrup. On top of this, put two scoops of each icecream, and top with the chopped almonds.

Not suitable for long-term freezing when made up.

Can be prepared 1 hour in advance, but sundaes won't sit around, so if you want to have them firm, pile the ingredients in the glasses and put them in the freezer until just before you want to eat them. But don't leave them for too long, and make sure that the glasses are strong enough to withstand the cold.

Cold

Coffee Pyramid

For the Icecream
3 egg yolks
3 dl. (½ pint) creamy milk
4 heaped tablespoons icing
  sugar
2–3 tablespoons boiling water
1 tablespoon instant coffee
3 dl. (½ pint) double cream

For the Sauce
8 tablespoons moist brown
  sugar

1 teaspoon cinnamon
8 tablespoons water

For the Meringues
3 egg whites
170 g. (6 oz.) castor sugar
pinch salt
1 teaspoon lard and 1
  tablespoon flour for
  preparing greaseproof paper

Preparation
Nil.

Action: Icecream

1. Pour the boiling water on to the coffee to dissolve it.
2. Heat the milk and icing sugar to scalding point, stirring to

179

make sure it dissolves. Mix in the coffee and withdraw the pan from the heat. Cool slightly.

3. When the milk is still quite warm, pour gradually on to the egg yolks and mix well. Cool completely and stir in the cream.

4. Pour into a freezing container and put into a freezer or freezing compartment of your refrigerator. Take out and beat several times while it is setting to break down the ice crystals.

Action: Meringues

5. Stiffly beat the egg whites with the salt, in a bowl completely free from grease. (This is very important.)

6. Beat in 1 tablespoon of the sugar, then add the rest of the sugar with a metal spoon, in two halves.

7. Lightly brush two sheets of greaseproof paper with melted lard, then dust with flour until the surface is lightly but completely covered. Place on baking sheets.

8. Either pipe small piles of the mixture on to the baking sheets, or drop from a spoon. Dust lightly with a little castor or icing sugar and leave to stand for 5 minutes.

9. Cook the meringues in a very slow oven for 1½ hours, or until they can easily be lifted off the baking sheets. Press the flat surface of the meringues to hollow them slightly, then replace upside down and continue cooking for 30 minutes. Cool, and if you are not going to use the meringues immediately store in an airtight tin.

Action: Sauce

10. Heat together the sugar, cinnamon and water and keep warm until required.

To complete

11. Sandwich together the meringues with blobs of the icecream. Make into a pyramid and serve the hot sauce separately.

Not suitable for freezing.

Can be prepared in advance until 10.

180

Cold

Ginger Chocolate Mousse

220 g. (½ lb.) bitter chocolate
3 tablespoons castor sugar
6 eggs
6 dessertspoons water

4 tablespoons ginger wine
3 pieces stem ginger (85 g.
(3 oz.) approx.)

Preparation

Separate the eggs. Finely chop the ginger.

Action

1. Heat together the chocolate, sugar and water until smooth.
2. Withdraw the pan from the heat and stir in the ginger wine. Allow to cool slightly, then stir in the egg yolks and pieces of ginger. Cool completely.
3. Whip the egg whites until stiff and fold into the chocolate mixture. Spoon into individual ramekins and chill until required.

Not suitable for freezing.

Can be prepared in advance.

Cold

Ginger Syllabub

6 dl. (1 pint) double cream
3 tablespoons castor sugar
8 dessertspoons green ginger
   wine

6 pieces stem ginger (140 g.
(5 oz.) (approx.)

Action

1. Whip together the cream and sugar, gradually blending in the ginger wine, continuing to whip until it is thick and fluffy.
2. Stir in the pieces of ginger. Spoon into individual glasses, and chill until required.

Not suitable for freezing.

Can be prepared in advance.

Cold

Caribbean Cream

9 dl. (1½ pints) commercially
   soured cream
6 tablespoons rum

6 tablespoons moist brown
   sugar

Preparation

Nil.

Action

Whip the sugar with the sour cream, and gradually beat in the
rum. Continue beating until well-aerated. Pour into individual
glasses and chill until required.

Not suitable for freezing.

Can be prepared in advance.

Cold

Crème Caramel

3 eggs
3 egg yolks
3 tablespoons castor sugar
¼ teaspoon (approx.) vanilla
   essence

9 dl. (1½ pints) milk
110 g. (5 oz.) castor sugar for
   caramel

Preparation

Nil.

Action

1. Heat the 110 g. (5 oz.) castor sugar in a small saucepan and
   melt without stirring until it begins to brown, then stir once or
   twice until it is a rich brown. Pour equal quantities into 8
   individual ramekins.
2. Mix together the eggs, the egg yolks, the other sugar and the
   vanilla essence, adding more to your taste if necessary.

182

3. Heat the milk to scalding point (hot but not boiling) and pour on to the eggs, whisking with a fork as you do so.

4. Pour the egg mixture on top of the caramel in the ramekins.

5. Stand the ramekins in a pan of water to come half way up the sides of the dishes. Cook in a moderate oven for 40 minutes or until the custard has set.

6. Cool and chill until required. Turn out on to individual plates before serving.

Not suitable for freezing.

Can be prepared in advance.

Cold

Crème Pots

3 dl. (½ pint) double cream
1½ dl. (¼ pint) milk
170 g. (6 oz.) castor sugar
3 dl. (½ pint) commercially
    soured cream

2 tablespoons Framboise
    liqueur or 1 teaspoon
    almond essence
2 heaped tablespoons gelatin
pinch salt
½ kg. (1 lb. 2 oz.) strawberries*

Preparation

Hull and clean the strawberries. Put the gelatin to soak with 1½ dl. (¼ pint) water.

Action

1. Place the double cream, milk, 110 g. (¼ lb.) of the sugar and the salt in a saucepan. Cook over a low heat, stirring constantly until the sugar has dissolved. Remove from heat and stir in the gelatin until completely dissolved, returning to the heat for a minute or two if necessary.

2. Transfer the contents of the pan to a bowl and blend in the soured cream and the Framboise or almond essence. Pour into individual ramekins and chill until firm.

3. Crush the strawberries with the rest of the sugar, adding a little more to taste if necessary.

4. At the point of service, turn the cream mixture out of the ramekins and pour over the strawberry sauce.

Suitable for freezing.

Can be prepared in advance keeping crème and sauce separate.

Note: Other fruits very good for the sauce are crushed raspberries or lightly stewed black or red currants.

Cold

Raspberry Marble

½ kg. (1 lb. 2 oz.) raspberries   4 dl. (⅔ pint) double cream
110 g. (¼ lb.) castor sugar   3 egg whites

Preparation

Whip the cream until thick.

Action

1. Lightly crush the raspberries (frozen will do) with the sugar.

2. Mix the cream with the fruit.

3. Whisk the egg whites until stiff and fold into the fruit, then
   pile into individual glasses. Chill until required.

Not suitable for freezing as such, but could be frozen and then
eaten as icecream, in which case a further 60 g. (2 oz.) sugar should
be added.

Can be prepared in advance.

Cold

Mango Fool

3 stringless mangoes   3 dl. (½ pint) double cream

Preparation

Cut the mangoes in half and remove the stones. Scoop the flesh out
from the skins. Whip the cream until thick.

184

Action

Purée the mango flesh with a fork and stir in the cream. Chill until required.

Not suitable for freezing.

Can be prepared a few hours in advance, but tastes a little metallic if left too long.

Cold

Gooseberry Cream

645 g. (1 lb. 3 oz.) gooseberries	2 level tablespoons gelatin
195 g. (7 oz.) castor sugar	6 dl. (1 pint) natural
8 tablespoons water	yoghourt

Preparation

Wash, top and tail gooseberries. Put the gelatin to soak with half the water.

Action

1. Place the gooseberries, sugar and the rest of the water in a saucepan and simmer gently over a low heat until the gooseberries are soft.
2. Withdraw the pan from the heat and stir in the gelatin until completely dissolved.
3. Push the contents of the pan through a sieve and leave to cool.
4. When cool, mix in the yoghourt. Pour the mixture into ramekins and leave to set in the refrigerator until required. The setting will take about 3 hours.

Not suitable for freezing.

Can be prepared in advance.

Cold

Lost Lover's Mousse

900 g. (2 lb.) greengages	3 dl. (½ pint) double cream
2 oranges	4 egg whites
170 g. (6 oz.) castor sugar	60 g. (2 oz.) shelled walnuts

Preparation

Wash the greengages. Finely grate the rind from the oranges and squeeze them.

Action

1. Place the greengages, sugar, orange peel and orange juice in a saucepan over a low heat and simmer gently for about 10 minutes, or until the greengages are soft.

2. Push the contents of the saucepan through a sieve, discarding the stones. Leave the purée to cool.

3. When the purée is cold, lightly beat the cream and stiffly beat the egg whites and fold into the purée. Stir in all but 8 walnut halves, which should be reserved for decoration.

4. Pour the purée into individual bowls and decorate each, when set, with the reserved walnuts. Chill until required.

Suitable for freezing.

Can be prepared in advance.

Cold

Orange Fluff

8 small oranges	85 g. (3 oz.) castor sugar
1 packet orange jelly	4 eggs
	6 tablespoons water

Preparation

Finely grate the rind from three of the oranges. Cut them all in half and cut out the flesh, as though you were preparing a grapefruit. Make sure all the pips and skin are removed. Separate the eggs.

Action

1. Heat the jelly with the water and dissolve. Cool.

2. Cream together the egg yolks and sugar. Mix into the jelly, then stir in the pieces of orange and the orange rind.

3. Stiffly beat the egg whites and fold into the mixture. Spoon into individual glasses and allow to set (2 hours). Chill until required.

Not suitable for freezing.

Can be prepared in advance.

Cold

Blackcurrant Snow

½ kg. (1 lb. 2 oz.) black-   6 egg whites
  currants   85 g. (3 oz.) castor sugar
140 g. (5 oz.) granulated sugar 2 tablespoons water

Preparation

Wash and de-string currants if necessary.

Action

1. Cook the currants with the granulated sugar and water in a saucepan over a low heat for 7 minutes, or until soft but not pulpy. Make sure the currants do not stick. Cool.

2. Whisk the egg whites with the castor sugar until stiff, then fold in the fruit.

3. Spoon into glasses and chill until required.

Not suitable for freezing.

Can be prepared a few hours in advance.

Note: Other puréed fruit could also be used if a different flavour and consistency is required.

Cold

Almond Apricots

¾ kg. (1 lb. 11 oz.) fresh   1 dl. (⅙ pint) water
  apricots   60 g. (2 oz.) flaked almonds
220 g. (½ lb.) granulated sugar

Preparation
Wash the apricots.

Action

1. Place the apricots in a saucepan with the sugar and water. Cover and simmer until soft, stirring occasionally to make sure the apricots are not sticking. They will take 10–15 minutes to cook.

2. When cooked, stone the apricots and put the flesh and juice into a blender (or Mouli, using the coarse disc) and give it a quick whisk, but don't make it too smooth—there should still be bits of apricot.

3. Cool and stir in the almonds. Serve with cream.

Suitable for freezing, if almonds are added after defrosting.

Can be prepared in advance, but stir in the almonds shortly before serving.

Cold

Tropical Salad

2 large pineapples   8 grenadillas (passion fruit)
1 large mango

Preparation

Cut the tops off the pineapples and reserve. Carefully cut out the flesh without piercing the skin. Extract the hard core and chop the rest of the flesh. Cut the mango in half and remove the stone. Scoop the flesh out of the skin and chop. Cut the tops off the grenadillas and scoop out the insides.

Action

Mix all the fruit together, put back into the pineapple shells and replace the tops. Chill until required.

Not suitable for freezing.

Can be prepared a few hours in advance.

Cold

Cultural Revolution

1 kg. (2¼ lb.) white grapes   1 tablespoon brown sugar
8 Chinese gooseberries

Preparation

Peel as many grapes as you can, but certainly more than half, and remove their pips. Peel and slice the Chinese gooseberries.

Action

Combine the fruit and sprinkle over the brown sugar. Chill.
Not suitable for freezing.
Can be prepared several hours in advance.

Cold

Home Leave

2 large grapefruit   670 g. (1½ lb.) raspberries
3 large eating pears   5 tablespoons castor sugar

Preparation

Put the grapefruit in water and bring quickly to the boil (this makes them easier to peel). Remove them and place in cold water. Peel and slice, removing any pips or pith. Peel, quarter and core the pears.

Action

Place the grapefruit in a bowl and sprinkle over the sugar. Add the pears and raspberries. Lightly mix the salad and chill.
Not suitable for freezing.
Can be prepared a few hours in advance.

Cold

Verandah Salad

4 large eating pears   900 g. (2 lb.) white grapes
3 grenadillas (passion fruit)   3 tablespoons castor sugar
2 peaches

Preparation

Peel, core and slice the pears. Peel the peaches by plunging them quickly into boiling water and then into cold; remove stones and slice the flesh. Peel and pip the grapes.

Action

1. Place the pears in a bowl. Scoop out the passion fruit and sieve the juice over the pears. Sprinkle over the sugar.

2. Add the peaches, then the grapes. Lightly mix and chill.

Not suitable for freezing.

Can be prepared a few hours in advance.

Cold

Sundown Salad

2 pineapples	220 g. ($\frac{1}{2}$ lb.) ripe red plums
4 oranges	3 tablespoons castor sugar

Preparation

Put the oranges in water and quickly bring to the boil. Remove them and place in cold water (this makes them easier to peel). Dip the plums quickly in the boiling water and place them in the cold water too. Peel the oranges and slice them. Skin the plums and remove their stones, cutting them in half.

Action

1. Peel and core the pineapples. Cut the fruit in semi-circles and place in a bowl. Squeeze the skin and core to extract as much juice as possible. Sprinkle with sugar.

2. Add the oranges, then the plums. Lightly mix the salad and chill.

Not suitable for freezing.

Can be prepared a few hours in advance.

Cold

Orange Salad

8 large oranges
4 tablespoons (approx.) castor
  sugar

1 miniature bottle Cointreau
  or Grand Marnier

Preparation

Peel the oranges very carefully, removing all pith. (This is most easily done if you place them in water and bring quickly to the boil, then immediately afterwards plunge them into cold water.)

Action

Slice the oranges and place in a glass dish in layers, sprinkling each layer with sugar and liqueur until all are used up. Chill in the refrigerator until required.

Suitable for freezing, but it will loose its fresh look.

Can be prepared a few hours in advance.

Cold

Strawberries with Raspberry Sauce

1 kg. (2¼ lb.) strawberries
335 g. (¾ lb.) raspberries
  (frozen will do)

1 miniature bottle Cointreau
sugar to taste if necessary
2 tablespoons icing sugar

Preparation

Clean and hull the strawberries, which can then be sliced if you prefer.

Action

1. Pour the Cointreau over the strawberries, with a little sugar if they are too sour. Leave for 2 hours.
2. Meanwhile purée the raspberries in a blender or Mouli, then sieve to get rid of pips. Mix well with the icing sugar.

N   191

3. At the point of service, pour the raspberry sauce over the strawberries.

Not suitable for freezing.

Can be prepared a few hours in advance.

Cold

Caramelized Grapefruit

6 grapefruit   9 dl. (1½ pints) water
220 g. (½ lb.) granulated sugar

Preparation

Cut the outer skin, paper thin, from three of the grapefruit. This is best done with a serrated knife, cutting towards you. There must be no white pith on the inside of the peel. Cut the peel into fine strips. Peel all the grapefruit, cutting through the pith to the flesh, so that no pith remains on the fruit. Discard the thick peel.

Action

1. Boil the sugar in the water, add the peel strips and simmer for 8 minutes.
2. Add the grapefruit. It is possible you may have a pan large enough to hold all the fruit at once, otherwise cook them in batches of two or three. They must be covered by the water. They should be simmered for 3 minutes each and removed from the water.
3. Reserve the water which still contains the fine strips of peel and slice the grapefruit. Some of the grapefruit will have too many pips to do this successfully or too much core. The core can be cut out prior to slicing, but if the grapefruit is too tough, it is better to remove the individual segments from the surrounding tissue. At least two grapefruit should be cut across in slices to make the dish look attractive.
4. Put the grapefruit into a serving dish and pour over the liquid, arranging the fine strips of peel on top. Chill until required.

Suitable for freezing.

Can be prepared in advance.

Cold

White Chocolate Peaches

12 ripe peaches   4 tablespoons Van Der Hum
335 g. (¾ lb.) white chocolate   liqueur
2 tablespoons water

Preparation

Peel the peaches by plunging them quickly into boiling water,
then into cold. Slice them into four quarters and remove the stones.
Place in individual bowls.

Action

1. Heat the chocolate with the water in a saucepan over a low heat
   until it melts.
2. Pour the liqueur over the peaches, then when the chocolate
   has cooled sufficiently not to crack your dishes, pour that over
   too. Chill until required.

Not suitable for freezing.

Can be prepared in advance.

Cold

Bourbon Bananas

12 ripe bananas   1½ dl. (¼ pint) Bourbon
4½ dl. (¾ pint) water   whisky
2 tablespoons golden syrup   1½ tablespoons icing sugar

Preparation

Peel and slice the bananas.

Action

1. Heat the water in a saucepan and mix in the syrup. Add the
   whisky and cool.
2. Put a sixth of the bananas into a shallow fireproof dish and
   cover with four tablespoons of the liquid. Sprinkle with the

icing sugar and put under a hot grill until the sugar has caramelized. Cool.

3. Put the remaining bananas in a serving dish and pour over the liquid. Carefully slide the caramelized bananas on to the top. Chill in the refrigerator.

Not suitable for freezing.

Can be prepared in advance.

Note: This dish is best when allowed to marinate in the refrigerator for 2 days.

Hot

Flaming Bananas

8 bananas	4 tablespoons castor sugar
2 lemons	1 miniature bottle banana
3 oranges	liqueur
110 g. (¼ lb.) butter	1 miniature bottle rum

Preparation

Squeeze the juice from the lemons and oranges. Peel the bananas and prick with a fork.

Action

1. Heat the butter in a large frying-pan. Place the bananas in it and sprinkle with half the sugar. Cook for 3 minutes, then turn the bananas, sprinkle with the rest of the sugar and pour over the fruit juice. Cook for a further 3 minutes, basting with the pan juices.

2. Pour over the liqueur and rum and warm thoroughly. Set light to the alcohol and carry, still flaming, to the table. Serve immediately with cream.

Not suitable for freezing.

Not suitable for advance preparation.

APPENDIX I
GENERAL INSTRUCTIONS

Pastry-Making

The art of successful pastry-making is to keep everything as cool as possible and to handle it no more than is necessary.

When covering a pie, you want to roll the pastry out to about 1·25 cm. (½ in.) wider all round than you need it. Cut off this surplus. Wet the rim of the pie-dish and make an edge all round the dish with the surplus pastry. Wet this again, then carefully pick up the main pastry, balancing it with the rolling-pin, and put it on top of the spare rim. Press the two pieces of pastry together, then hold the pie-dish and cut round the edge (from the bottom) with a knife. With the pastry that is left over you can make whatever decorations you like to go on top. You should always make an incision in the pie top somewhere to allow the steam to escape. Brushing the pastry with a lightly beaten raw egg before baking will give it a glazed look and will help to prevent it going soggy.

When the recipe calls for you to bake a flan case blind, you should spread a sheet of greaseproof paper over the bottom of the flan case, and cover this with dried beans or rice to hold the pastry down. When the flan has been cooked for the appropriate time, the paper and beans should be lifted out and stored for further use for this purpose.

All pastry may be successfully frozen.

Shortcrust Pastry

The ingredients are plain flour, fat, a pinch of salt and a little cold water. For shortcrust pastry allow half the quantity of fat to flour. Therefore if you have 220 g. (½ lb.) flour, you will need 110 g. (¼ lb.) butter, or a mixture of half margarine and half lard. Butter makes a much richer pastry; margarine and lard make a lighter one.

Action

1. Sieve the flour into a bowl. Add the salt and the fat. Cut the fat into pieces with your knife to avoid handling.

2. Rub the fat into the flour with your thumbs and finger-tips until the mixture resembles breadcrumbs.

3. Add the cold water, a few drops at a time and mix with a knife. You will need approximately 3 tablespoons of water per 220 g. ($\frac{1}{2}$ lb.) flour. When the mixture is just damp enough to bind together you will have the right consistency, and you can now put it on a floured board and roll out to the required size.

Suitable for freezing.

Note: If you want to freeze the pastry, simply roll it into a block of suitable size so that it is easy to pack and will defrost more quickly than if left in a ball. It will take about 3 hours to defrost at room temperature.

Rich Shortcrust Pastry

The ingredients and method of making are basically the same as those for ordinary shortcrust pastry. However, the fat should always be all butter, and the liquid made up of 1 egg yolk mixed with 2 dessertspoons of water per 220 g. ($\frac{1}{2}$ lb.) flour. One dessert-spoon of castor sugar should always be added after the fat has been rubbed into the flour and before the liquid is added. With these amendments, the directions for making ordinary shortcrust pastry should be followed.

Flaky Pastry

The ingredients are plain flour, fat, a pinch of salt, $\frac{1}{2}$ teaspoon lemon juice per 220 g. ($\frac{1}{2}$ lb.) of flour, and a little cold water (2 tablespoons approx.).

For flaky pastry, allow three-quarters the quantity of fat to flour. Therefore if you have 220 g. ($\frac{1}{2}$ lb.) flour you will need 170 g. (6 oz.) fat. This is usually made up of half lard and half butter or margarine.

Action

1. Thoroughly mix together on a plate the butter or margarine and lard, then divide into four equal portions.

2. Sieve the flour into the bowl with a pinch of salt.

3. Put a quarter of the fat into the bowl with the flour and rub it in with the thumbs and finger-tips.

4. Add the lemon juice and the water a little at a time to form an elastic paste, mixing all the time with a knife.

5. Put the paste on to a floured board, roll it out in the shape of a long rectangle, and mark it lightly with a knife into three equal portions.

6. Put blobs of the second portion of fat on to the top two-thirds you have marked out on the pastry. Fold the pastry over in thirds, first folding the bottom section up, then the top section down over that. Seal the edges with the rolling-pin. Turn the pastry once round to the left so that the fold is on the left and roll it out again into the rectangle.

7. Mark the pastry into three again and repeat the procedure with the third quarter of the fat. Turn it again once to the left and roll out as before.

8. Repeat the procedure with the last quarter of the fat, turning it once to the left again.

9. When all the fat is used up, roll the pastry out once more, mark it into three and fold it again. Seal the edges with the rolling-pin, then put the pastry as it is in the refrigerator for at least 2 hours. After this period you can roll it out and use as directed.

Suitable for freezing.

Cheese Pastry

The ingredients are plain flour, butter, a mixture of Parmesan and Cheddar cheese, an egg yolk, pepper, salt and cayenne pepper, plus a little water.

For 220 g. ($\frac{1}{2}$ lb.) flour allow 170 g. (6 oz.) butter, 170 g. (6 oz.)

mixed grated Parmesan and Cheddar cheese, 1 large egg yolk, 2 tablespoons water, salt, pepper and a pinch of cayenne pepper.

Action

1. Sieve the flour with the salt, pepper and cayenne into a bowl. Cut the butter into pieces and drop into the flour, seeing that each piece becomes well coated with flour.
2. With the thumbs and finger-tips rub the fat into the flour until the mixture resembles breadcrumbs.
3. Add the grated cheeses and stir in with a knife.
4. Mix the egg yolk with the water, then tip into the bowl with the other ingredients and mix with a knife.
5. Turn on to a floured board and knead lightly until it is smooth. Put into the refrigerator for at least 30 minutes before rolling out. After this period it may be rolled out and used as directed.

Suitable for freezing.

Seasoned Flour

This is used for coating meat before frying. When a recipe calls for seasoned flour, you should mix salt and pepper, and any of the herbs recommended for the particular recipe, with the flour. The easiest and least messy way of coating meat in seasoned flour is to put the flour in a large polythene bag, drop the meat into it and shake the bag until the meat is completely coated with the flour.

Stock

With the exception of the recipes calling for a strong stock, stock made with a chicken or meat cube can be substituted for the real thing—for which recipes are given below. (When mild stock is called for, a chicken cube dissolved in water is suitable.) However, if you are doing a lot of cooking, it is well worth having a 'stock pot'. Good stock will keep in a very cool place for up to a week, but in warm weather it is necessary to boil it up every two days. All stock may be frozen.

Chicken Stock

To the bones and carcass of a cooked chicken, with giblets if available, add 1 sliced carrot, 2 sticks celery, 1 onion stuck with 3 cloves, parsley, a sprig of thyme and a bayleaf tied together, a wedge of lemon, 1 teaspoon salt, 6 peppercorns and 9 dl. (1½ pints) water. Put all the ingredients in a heavy saucepan, bring to the boil and skim off the scum. Turn the heat down to low, cover the pan and simmer for 2½–3 hours. Strain into a bowl. Allow to cool and remove any fat before using.

Meat Stock

To 1–1¼ kg. (2¼–2¾ lb.) of meat bones (these can be beef, lamb, veal or pork, but probably the best are beef and veal), add 4 stalks celery, 2 onions each stuck with 2 cloves, 1 sliced carrot, parsley, a sprig of thyme and a bayleaf tied together, 2 teaspoons salt, 8 peppercorns, 1¼–1½ litres (2–3 pints) water. Put all the ingredients in a heavy saucepan, bring to the boil and skim off the scum. Turn the heat down to low, cover the pan and simmer for 2½–3 hours. When the stock is cooked, strain it into a bowl. Allow to cool and remove any fat before using.

Glazing with Aspic

The recipes in this book which call for glazing with aspic bear the instructions 'Make up the aspic following the directions on the packet'. We say this because we feel it unrealistic to expect people to make their own aspic, as it is a fairly long and expensive process. Having said that, however, we feel we could give you some helpful advice on how to achieve the best and smoothest results with your aspic.

The first thing to remember is that the dish to be glazed must be completely cold and have as smooth a surface as possible. The aspic too should be quite cold, and *just* beginning to set. You should then spoon a thin layer of the aspic over the dish to be glazed and allow this to set—the quickest way of doing this is to put it in the freezing compartment of the refrigerator for about 5 minutes. Bring the dish out, and garnish it in any way you like, making it as light and attractive as possible. Spoon on another very thin layer of the aspic, just sufficient to cover the decoration, and allow this to set. When this second layer has set, spoon over the rest of the aspic, and leave this to set. In the case of moulds where you are setting such things as prawns in aspic, and it is necessary to turn out the mould at the end, the easiest method is to plunge the bowl into a bowl of hand-hot water, then wipe the edges so that the water does not drip on to the food as it is turned out. Turn the mould upside down on the serving plate and shake very gently. If it does not move at once, plunge into the water once more and try again.

APPENDIX II
SAUCES AND ACCOMPANIMENTS

Mayonnaise
(by hand)

The ingredients for an average quantity of mayonnaise are 2 egg yolks, 1 level teaspoon made mustard, 1 level teaspoon salt, $\frac{1}{2}$ level teaspoon castor sugar, plenty of freshly ground black pepper, 3 dl. ($\frac{1}{2}$ pint) oil, 2–3 teaspoons wine vinegar or lemon juice.

Action

1. Put the egg yolks into a bowl and add the mustard, salt, sugar and pepper. Mix well together.
2. Measure the oil out into a jug and add it to the egg yolks, drop by drop, beating all the time with a whisk until it begins to thicken. After this it may be added a little faster, but not much (a good method is to let the oil trickle very gently down the side of the bowl), otherwise the mayonnaise will curdle. Should this happen, break another egg yolk into a fresh bowl and mix with a little made mustard, then gradually beat the thin mayonnaise into the yolk.
3. When the oil is all used up and the mayonnaise is really thick, add a little vinegar or lemon juice to thin it to the right consistency. Adjust seasoning if necessary.

Not suitable for freezing.

Note: Mayonnaise will keep in a screw-top jar in the refrigerator for at least a week. (The keeping quality of mayonnaise is slightly improved by the final addition of 1 tablespoon of boiling water.)

Mayonnaise
(with an electric blender)

The ingredients for this type of mayonnaise are slightly different in that you can use one whole egg, rather than two egg yolks. Other ingredients are exactly the same as in the previous recipe.

Action

1. Put the whole egg into the blender with the sugar, seasoning, mustard and vinegar or lemon juice. Switch on to fast, and mix.
2. Keeping the blender switched to fast, pour in the oil in a thin stream. Immediately it starts to thicken, add the rest of the oil more quickly.
3. If, when all the oil is used up, the mayonnaise appears to be too thick, add a little more vinegar or lemon juice.

Not suitable for freezing.

French Dressing

The classical recipe for French dressing is 3 parts oil to 1 part vinegar, a good pinch of salt and freshly ground black pepper. However, most people have their own variations on this recipe, and two of ours are given below. Use a well-flavoured olive oil or any other salad oil you prefer.

French dressing keeps well in a bottle in the refrigerator, and it is often useful to have some on hand, and we therefore recommend that you make fairly large quantities at a time.

French Dressing No. 1

5 parts oil to 1 part wine vinegar, 1 clove of garlic, ½ teaspoon made mustard, 1 teaspoon sugar. The ingredients other than the oil and vinegar would be sufficient for 2 dl. (⅓ pint), but alter the other ingredients to suit your own taste. Mix together the mustard, sugar and oil, then stir in the vinegar, salt and pepper. Transfer to a screw-top bottle, put the peeled whole clove of garlic into the dressing, and leave for 24 hours for the flavour to develop.

French Dressing No. 2

4 parts oil to 1 part wine vinegar, 1 clove garlic, 1 tablespoon each of finely chopped parsley, tarragon, chervil and chives, * seasoning.

Chop the herbs and garlic finely. Combine with the oil, add the vinegar, salt and freshly ground black pepper.

Note: Dried herbs *can* be used but are not nearly so satisfactory.

Oil and Vinegar Dressing

Crush 6 cloves of garlic and place them in a screw-top jar with ½ litre (⅚ pint) finest Italian salad oil, a little salt and pepper and 2 tablespoons vinegar. Shake well before using.

White Sauce

The ingredients are butter, flour, milk or some other liquid (better warmed, but this is not essential), and seasoning (see note for quantities).

Action

1. Heat the butter in a saucepan large enough to hold the total quantity of liquid being used.
2. When the butter has melted, but not browned, withdraw the pan from the heat and stir in the flour. Return to the heat and cook the mixture over a low heat for 2 minutes, stirring all the time.
3. Withdraw the pan from the heat again and mix in the liquid very slowly, stirring all the time to avoid lumps.
4. When all the liquid is blended in, return the pan to the heat and bring gently to the boil, stirring constantly as it thickens. If by chance you find yourself with a lumpy-looking sauce, whisk it furiously just before it comes to the boil—once it has boiled it is too late, and then the only thing to do is sieve it.
5. Once the sauce has come to the boil, continue cooking gently and stirring for 4 minutes, then withdraw the pan from the heat and stir in the seasoning.

Notes: The thickness of the sauce depends on the ratio of fat and flour to liquid. To get a very thick sauce you will need less liquid proportionately to fat and flour, whereas to get a thin sauce you will need more. For a very thin sauce the quantities are 30 g. (1 oz.) butter, 30 g. (1 oz.) flour to 6 dl. (1 pint) liquid; for a slightly thicker sauce, 60 g. (2 oz.) butter, 60 g. (2 oz.) flour to 6 dl. (1 pint) liquid; and for a thick sauce 85 g. (3 oz.) butter, 85 g. (3 oz.) flour to 6 dl. (1 pint) liquid.

Increasing the ratio of butter to flour in a white sauce produces a richer consistency.

Suitable for freezing.

Can be prepared in advance.

Brown Sauce

The ingredients are butter or dripping, flour, stock (better warmed, but this is not essential), an onion, a small piece of carrot, and seasoning.

Action

1. Skin and finely chop the onion and carrot. Heat the butter or dripping in a saucepan and fry the vegetables for 5 minutes. Sprinkle over the flour and continue cooking, stirring constantly for 7 minutes, or until the flour is a rich brown.

2. Gradually blend in the stock. Bring to the boil, stirring constantly. Season well. Cover the pan and continue to simmer for 30 minutes, stirring occasionally and skimming off the fat when necessary.

3. When cooked, strain and use as directed.

Suitable for freezing.

Can be prepared in advance.

Hollandaise Sauce

The ingredients for an average quantity of hollandaise sauce are as follows: 5 egg yolks, 195 g. (7 oz.) butter, 3 tablespoons water and seasoning.

Action

1. Put the egg yolks, water and a little seasoning in the top half of a double saucepan, or bowl, over hot, but not boiling water. Stir rapidly over the water until the mixture begins to thicken.

2. When this happens, immediately remove the mixture from the heat and add half the butter, cut into small pieces. Put back over the water and stir constantly with a wire beater. As the butter melts, the sauce becomes creamy.

3. When this happens, remove from the water and add the rest of the butter. Return once more to the hot water and continue stirring. When the sauce thickens it is ready. Serve immediately.

Not suitable for freezing.

Not suitable for advance preparation.

Note: Be very careful not to allow the water beneath the sauce to boil, because the sauce can very easily scramble or curdle.

Béarnaise Sauce

The ingredients for an average quantity of béarnaise sauce are as follows: 5 egg yolks, 195 g. (7 oz.) butter, 2 shallots, 3 tablespoons wine vinegar, 2 tablespoons water, 1 teaspoon tarragon, seasoning.

Action

1. Peel the shallots and finely chop. Wash the tarragon if using fresh, which is best and chop.

2. Place the shallots and vinegar in an open pan over a moderate heat for 10 minutes, by which time the vinegar will have been reduced by half or more. Put through a sieve.

3. Now put the vinegar and water in the top of a double saucepan, together with the egg yolks, tarragon and seasoning, then follow the directions for hollandaise sauce above.

Not suitable for freezing.

Can be prepared in advance when served cold.

APPENDIX III

BASIC NOTES ON FREEZING

It will have been seen that all the recipes in this book are marked as to whether or not they can be successfully frozen. It is therefore appropriate to have a few basic notes on freezing. Since our last book, *Freeze Now, Dine Later*, is totally devoted to home freezing, we wish to keep the advice in this book to a bare minimum, and to confine ourselves to purely practical notes on the circumstances you will encounter when freezing, defrosting and reheating made-up dishes. Below are 10 basic rules to freezing which we hope you will find a practical and useful guide.

1. Only freeze the best and freshest foods. Good-quality food comes out of the freezer as it goes in. The same applies to inferior food. *Remember! There is no magic in the freezer. The good is well preserved, but the poor is not improved.* You can freeze almost anything, but below is a list of those items we consider for one reason or another are either unsatisfactory or not worth freezing:

(a) Most salad vegetables—lettuce, watercress, chicory. They become limp and desiccated as though frost-bitten. Tomatoes, although useful for incorporating in cooked dishes, are no good as a salad vegetable as they go soft.

(b) Bananas and avocado pears. Texture is destroyed and flavour impaired.

(c) New potatoes. Although these are now frozen commercially, we consider there is too great a loss of texture to make freezing worthwhile.

(d) Single cream, yoghourt, sour cream, mayonnaise, hollandaise and béarnaise sauces. These separate, but may be incorporated in small quantities in dishes.

(e) Eggs in their shells. Shells crack through expansion. But eggs can be successfully frozen if removed from their shells. Whites can be frozen on their own, but yolks should have either a teaspoon of salt or sugar added per half dozen eggs, depending

on whether they are to be used for sweet or savoury purposes. If yolks and whites are mixed they should also have this addition, but do remember to label them clearly as to whether salt or sugar has been added. Hard-boiled eggs go rubbery.
(f) Vanilla essence. Flavour impaired.
(g) Meringues. Soft varieties leak.

2. Ensure that the freezer is kept at a constant maximum temperature of 0 degrees F. (− 18 degrees C.), and that there is plenty of air circulation around it. You can keep a freezer almost anywhere, but it should not be subjected to extremes of heat or cold.

3. Ensure that food is correctly wrapped in the quantities most suitable for future use. It is always easier to use two portions than to try and separate four portions from a solidly frozen block of food intended for eight. Make sure the packages are completely airtight and correctly labelled. It is all too easy to think that you can't possibly forget that the irregular shaped packet contains chicken—you can! Correct packaging is extremely important and it preserves frozen food in perfect condition.

There are many forms of freezer containers available on the market, but probably the most useful is the polythene bag. These are cheap, readily available and convenient for awkward shapes. They do tear fairly easily, so sharp bone ends should be wrapped in freezer paper or foil to prevent them puncturing the bags. Aluminium foil is also extremely useful, as are plastic containers. The latter are particularly good for liquids, and can be used over and over again.

Oven glassware and casseroles make effective containers and have the great advantage of being suitable for serving from, at the table. There is always a slight risk that a casserole may crack if put straight from the freezer into a cold oven and immediately heated, but this has never been our experience. If ovenware is to be put in the freezer, then seal around the top of the lid with freezer tape. Alternatively place without a lid in a polythene bag, extracting the air through a straw. The disadvantage of using ovenware for freezing is that it will be out of circulation for the period of freezing. To avoid this, the casserole can be lined with heavy-duty foil and then the package lifted out when frozen. When you come

o   207

to use the food the frozen shape will suggest the dish you originally used, and, after removing the wrappings, you can place the contents back in the same dish.

4. Food should be handled as little as possible before freezing, and frozen as quickly as possible after it has been prepared and cooled.

5. Ensure that the freezer can't be accidentally switched off. It is a good idea to stick a piece of sellotape over the plug so that the switch can't be turned off, either by children or by over-zealous preservers of electricity. It is a good idea to put a notice by the mains switch reminding you not to turn off the whole system when you go away on holiday.

6. There is very little to go wrong with a freezer, and most faults are located in the plug or switch. If it does go off don't open the freezer door even if you are tempted to peer in to see what is going on. Cover the freezer with blankets or newspapers to insulate it, and call a mechanic immediately. The food will remain completely frozen for 8 hours, and by then the fault should have been corrected. Even if it hasn't, the food won't go bad, but will keep in the freezer for a day. However, if you know that food has been defrosted for a period, try to use it up fairly quickly.

7. Don't use your freezer as a long-term refrigerator for preserving unwanted scraps of food, or for hoarding foods you don't particularly like, but hope might come in useful. Don't leave seasonable foods in the freezer so long that you are eating them when the season returns.

8. Keep a regular turnover of food. Always bring the bottom packages up to the top. If you have the energy, it is a good idea to keep a chart of the food the freezer contains, and keep it up to date, and you will never be caught out by unexpected guests.

9. Don't overload the freezer with unfrozen food. Only add 10 per cent of the freezer's total capacity in 24 hours.

10. Remember most herbs and seasonings react differently in frozen dishes. Most herb flavours tend to become stronger, particularly that of bayleaves, and these should be used sparingly, and removed before the dish is frozen. Garlic has a reputation for

developing an off taste, but we have not found this. The flavour of salt tends to disappear and should be added again if necessary before serving.

Freezing Life of Composite Dishes

The object of freezing foods is to preserve for your needs, rather than to store indefinitely. With a regular turnover of the frozen dishes in your freezer you will probably find that you are keeping a dish frozen on average from 2–3 months.

We have eaten dishes which we froze as long as a year before, so the following table is simply a guide to help you to understand the limits within which you should eat your frozen dishes so as to be certain of the best results.

Dishes containing beef, chicken, game and lamb	6–9 months
Dishes containing pork, offal, turkey, goose, duck and veal	3–6 months
Dishes containing fish	3 months
Flans, cakes, puddings and bread	3 months

The above chart relates to food kept at the recommended storage temperature of 0 degrees F. (− 18 degrees C.).

Defrosting and Reheating Frozen Dishes

If frozen dishes are not to be placed straight from the freezer into a cold oven, it is better to defrost them in the refrigerator, still sealed. The slow defrosting allows the food juices to be easily reabsorbed. However, in the case of cakes not to be served chilled, room temperature is more satisfactory. Decorated cakes and puddings should have their wrappings loosened during defrosting to prevent damage. Heavy foil impedes defrosting and an extra time allowance should be made for foods wrapped in foil. Food should remain sealed to prevent oxygen causing discolouration, to prevent dehydration, to guard against food becoming tainted by strong flavours in the refrigerator and for reasons of hygiene.

It is difficult to be accurate about precise times for defrosting since so many factors have to be taken into consideration. However, if you follow the general rule of allowing 7–10 hours per ½ kg. (1 lb. approx.) in a domestic refrigerator and 3–4 hours at room temperature, you will not go too far wrong. It is a good idea to start the defrosting overnight in the refrigerator, then if the defrosting needs to be speeded up it can be brought into room temperature for a few hours.

It is not necessary to defrost stews at all since the juices can be reabsorbed, but the dish will take about twice as long to reheat. It does help though if you stir a frozen casserole from time to time, and if you are short of time the dish can be reheated quite quickly on top of the stove. Remember to check seasonings after defrosting.

When reheating frozen dishes, they should be brought to bubbling point and left there for 10 minutes.

INDEX

211